NUMEROLOGY

———◆———

Quodque est innumerum, numero comprehendere

HEIRIC, *Vita Sancti Germani*, VI. 279

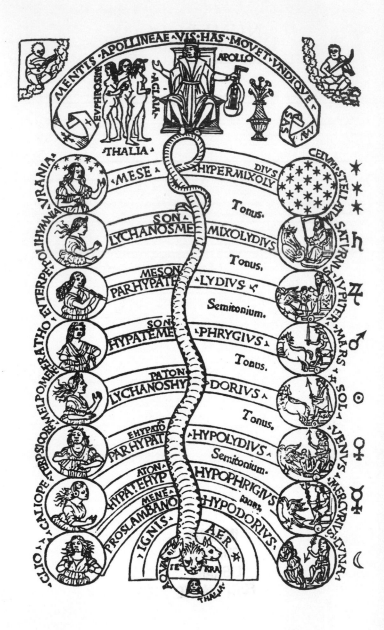

NUMEROLOGY

Theory and outline history of a literary mode

JOHN MACQUEEN

EDINBURGH UNIVERSITY PRESS

© J. MacQueen 1985
Edinburgh University Press
22 George Square, Edinburgh

Set in Monotype Poliphilus
by Speedspools, Edinburgh

Printed in Great Britain by
Kingprint of Richmond, Surrey

British Library Cataloguing
    in Publication Data
MacQueen, John
Numerology
1. Symbolism of numbers in literature.
I. Title
809   PN56.S9

ISBN 0 85224 492 4

8   4/23/86

Contents

Preface

This little book for the most part limits itself to the Western tradition, and even there its coverage is highly selective. The emphasis on Scottish, and Irish material is a deliberate attempt to show their significance for the development of the mode.

I am grateful to students and colleagues in Edinburgh and elsewhere with whom over the years I have discussed numero‑logical analysis. I should also like to thank Mr Archie Turnbull, Mrs L. Jones and Mr John M. Davidson of Edinburgh Univer‑sity Press for the help and advice which they willingly extended to me. The faults of the book are, of course, my own.

Now that it is completed, I should like to inscribe the book 'For Angus and the visual abstract'.

School of Scottish Studies
2 October 1984

1

Acrostics, numbers and the Bible

Genesis—Revelation—Voyage of St Brendan

In a celebrated passage, the Roman writer on architecture, Vitruvius,[1] who probably lived in the latter part of the first century B C, maintained that a vital relationship existed between architectural proportions and those of the human body, which in turn echoed the divine proportions of the universe. He took for granted the notion, universal from antiquity to the Renaissance and beyond, that man as microcosm is himself an image, even a summary, of macrocosmic perfections.[2] As an architect, Vitruvius laid special emphasis on the proportions appropriate to temples, dedicated to the gods who rule the macrocosm. The symmetry of the human body reflects that of creation by way of certain numbers—10, 6 and 16—together with certain ratios and geometrical figures—1:10, 1:8, 1:6, 1:4, 1:3, the circle, the square. Architectural proportions are derived from those of the body; 10 is important, but 6 in a sense more so, because it contains in itself and generates more ratios, including those which, as will be shown in chapter two, form the basis of ancient and medieval musical theory, and were important in cosmological speculation:

> The mathematicians, however, maintaining a different view, have said that the perfect number is six, because this number is composed of integral parts which are suited numerically to their method of reckoning: thus one is one sixth; two is one third; three is one half; four is two thirds, or $\delta i\mu o\iota\rho o\varsigma$ as they call it; five is five sixths, called $\pi\epsilon\nu\tau\acute{a}\mu o\iota\rho o\varsigma$; and six is

the perfect number. As the number goes on growing larger, the addition of a unit above six is the ἔφεκτος; eight, formed by the addition of a third part of six, is the integer and a third, called ἐπίτριτος; the addition of one half makes nine, the integer and a half, called ἡμιόλιος; the addition of two thirds, making the number ten, is the integer and two thirds, which they call ἐπιδίμοιρος; in the number eleven, where five are added, we have the five sixths, called ἐπίπεμπτος; finally, twelve, being composed of the two simple integers, is called διπλάσιος. [*De architectura*, 3.1.6.]

The best procedure for the architect is to link the separate perfections of 6 and 10, and base his designs on 16, the sum of 10 and 6.

The passage clearly implies a link between music and the visual and plastic arts. But the relationship is even more extensive, as may be illustrated by a passage in the metrical *Life of Germanus*, composed by the Carolingian poet Heiric (c.840–c.876), and quoted in chapter three below.[3] Although there can be no direct connection, this apparently echoes Vitruvius, but applies the concept of 6 as a perfect and generative number to literary composition. The poem represents a later development, but when it is taken into account as naturally rising from the cluster of ideas already present, Vitruvius may be said to imply, to a degree probably unimaginable to his own contemporaries, that numbers, ratios and geometric figures link the arts generally, by way of the microcosm, to the macrocosm:

> Therefore, if it is agreed that number was found out from the human fingers, and that there is a symmetrical correspondence between the members separately and the entire form of the body, in accordance with a certain part selected as standard, we can have nothing but respect for those who, in constructing temples of the immortal gods, have so arranged the members of the works that both the separate parts and the whole design may harmonize in their proportions and symmetry. [*3.1.9*]

No one today queries the existence or the importance of

numerically based symmetries in architecture, in the visual and plastic arts, and in music. Only in literature is the situation different. The concept has been resisted, and the hybrid term numerology, or numerological analysis, coined for it, has not yet fully achieved its place in the English critical vocabulary. It made no appearance, for instance, in Roger Fowler's *A Dictionary of Modern Critical Terms* (1973), while *The Fontana Dictionary of Modern Thought* (ed. Bullock and Stallybrass, 1977), included only the adjectival form in the entry *numerological criticism*, defined pejoratively as 'an ambitious attempt to apply number symbol/logy to literary works'. In this latter, present/day critical interest is said to derive substantially from Vincent Hopper's *Medieval Number Symbolism* (1938), from Edgar Wind's *Pagan Mysteries in the Renaissance* (1958) and G. Duckworth's *Structural Patterns and Proportions in Vergil's Aeneid* (1962); to take as its exemplar Kent Hieatt's *Short Time's Endless Monument* (1960), a study of Spenser's *Epithalamion*, but 'as now understood', to begin with Alastair Fowler's *Spenser and the Numbers of Time* (1964). The entry closes dismissively, 'Numerological criticism is by no means universally recognised as valid or important'.

The references are factually accurate, but the omissions are more notable than the inclusions. Scholarship has recognised the importance of literary numerology, at least in some areas, for much longer than is suggested. The numerological element in Dante's poetry, for instance, was rediscovered in the early years of this century.[4] 'Rediscovered' is the appropriate word; there is plenty of evidence that readers in earlier centuries recognised the importance of numerical patterns in terms of literary structure and philosophic or theological meaning. The entry gives no hint of this earlier concern, or of the extent of the European cultural background. Even within the period covered, there is no refer/ence to such seminal works as E. R. Curtius's *European Literature and the Latin Middle Ages* (1948; English translation, 1953), Johannes Alphonsus Huisman's *Neue Wege zur dichterischen und musikalischen Technik Walthers von der Vogelweide, Mit einen Exkurs über die symmetrische Zahlenkomposition im Mittelalter* (1950), Gunnar Qvarnström's *Dikten och Den Nya Vetenskapen* (1961), and Maren-Sofie Røstvig's *The Hidden Sense* (1963). The subject, in short, is better established, more extensive, and much more important than the Fontana *Dictionary* would seem to indicate.

Literary numerology may be defined as the theory of verse and prose composition in terms of which an author deliberately incorporates in the text of his work numerical patterns which he regards as conveying precise significances. The first literary numerologists, that is to say, were story-tellers and poets rather than modern academic analysts. The earliest and most influential, it will become clear in the course of this chapter, were the Hebrew authors of some parts of the Old Testament. In the early Christian centuries the compositional principles which they adopted were expanded to include Greek ideas of number, largely derived from Pythagorean and Platonic sources. At least in the best examples the patterns obtained are structurally meaningful as well as ornamental, and thus help to clarify the attentive reader's perception of detail and development. In a poem, the number of lines or stanzas is usually involved; in a prose work, the number of chapters or books: in either, the groups of characters who appear, the names which they are given, the number of incidents which takes place, the length of time occupied by single episodes and the entire action, may help to establish the mould. On the whole, a wider, more complex and more delicate range of effects is open to the poet than to the prose writer.

Although the ultimate origin is biblical, and many later developments derive from Greek sources, the multiple senses of the Latin word *numerus*—'number', 'musical measure', 'harmony', 'verse'—may have contributed to the development of numerological theory and practice. Augustine of Hippo's *De Musica* was certainly an important influence in this respect.[5]

E. R. Curtius did not use the term numerology, but in effect saw the technique as part of a more extended system to describe which he coined the phrase 'numerical composition' (*zahlenkomposition*).[6] As he noted, the numerical patterns involved may be very simple, consisting of nothing more than 'a predilection for round numbers (50, 100, 200)', or more complicated, especially when symbolic numbers—5, 7, 9 and many others believed to have a philosophic or theological significance—are involved. Numerology is too elaborate a term for the first, but for the second the phrase 'numerological composition' might be more appropriate.

This book is an attempt not merely to analyse specimens of numerological composition, but to indicate, so far as may be possible, the general basis for the kind—an attempt handicapped by the fact that while there are many expositions of the significance of individual numbers, the principles underlying the applications of numbers to composition tend to remain assumed rather than expressed. To attach significance to numbers is by no means the same as to make numbers the basis of composition. I have attempted throughout to keep this distinction in mind.

Analysis is complicated by the fact that during antiquity and the greater part of the Middle Ages letters and numerals had no separate notation. Numbers were expressed by letters, to all appearance arbitrarily chosen, but nevertheless suggesting a close relationship between the elements of number and those of coherent utterance. The Romans had I for 1 (*unus*), V for 5 (*quinque*), X for 10 (*decem*), L for 50 (*quinquaginta*), D for 500 (*quingenti*). Only in C for 100 (*centum*) and M for 1000 (*mille*) is there a direct relation between alphabetic symbol and numerical significance. But at least the arbitrary correspondences are relatively simple. This however was not always the case: the relationship often embodied extra layers of meaning, sometimes involving assumed supernatural qualities in the letters themselves. In the Hellenistic period, the Greeks, who already used their alphabet to represent numerals, saw a mysterious correspondence between the fact that their alphabet possessed seven vowel signs (α, ε, η, ι, o, υ, ω) and the existence of the seven pre-Copernican planets whose influences were believed to dominate the entire sublunary world. Gilbert Murray wrote: 'The vowels are the mystic signs of the planets; they have control over the planets. Hence strange prayers and magic formulae innumerable'.[7]

In the thirteenth century, the combinatory Art of Ramon Lull (1235–1315)[8] depended on the representation of the nine

Dignities of God by the nine letters which follow A (God himself) in the alphabet, B C D E F G H I K. Most problems, it was
held, were capable of solution by appropriate combinations of
the letters. Conventions in many ways similar survive to the
present. The principal weapon of algebra, for instance, is the
generalised representation of numbers by letters, for instance
$(a+b)^2 = a^2 + 2ab + b^2$. Letters from the beginning of the
alphabet are used to represent known or given numbers, letters
from the end to represent unknown but ascertainable numbers.
The arbitrary order of letters in the alphabet is almost as important
for algebra as for Lull's Art; it is still more important, and has
not lost its links with number, in the statement given to Christ
by the author of *Revelation*,[9] 'I am Alpha and Omega, the
beginning and the ending'.

One feature is especially characteristic of languages such as
Hebrew and Greek in which the entire alphabet was used to form
numerical expressions. Every word as well as every letter—
indeed, any sequence of letters, however long—thus had
numerical values, which might be calculated by a variety of
methods. The process might be applied to words or texts of any
kind, most often however to personal names. In *Genesis 14.14*
Abram took 318 trained servants, born in his own house, with
him to defeat Ched-or-la-o-mer, King of Elam, with his allies,
and so rescue Lot, his nephew. 318 men are clearly regarded
as constituting a formidable force, but why is the number chosen
in preference to a round figure such as 300 or 350? '318 is the sum
of the consonants of the name of Abram's steward Eliezer in its
original Hebrew form. The number is apparently constructed
from the name.'[10] The explanation is convincing, despite the
fact that Eliezer's name first appears only in the succeeding
chapter. It is there implied however that he is a person of great
importance, described as Abram's heir-presumptive, though a
slave, a position which he retains until the birth of Isaac. It is
also likely that Eliezer is the 'eldest servant of his house, that ruled
over all that he had' [*Genesis 24.2*], whom Abram, now
Abraham, many years later sent to the city of Nahor in Mesopotamia to obtain a wife for Isaac from his own kindred. The

version of the Abraham saga preserved in *Genesis* would seem to have been condensed and partly reshaped from an earlier one in which the part of Eliezer was more prominent, and in which the number indicated by the letters of his name was more likely to cross the reader's threshold of attention. A form of numerical composition derived from alphabetical sources, it is thus possible to say, has affected the shape, the development of the saga.

Almost the same might be said of the change of name from Abram to Abraham [*Genesis 17.5*], explicable on similar grounds, but also introducing a new idea, that of the power inherent in a particular number. In *The Garden of Cyrus or, The Quincunciall, Lozenge, or Net-Work Plantations of the Ancients, Artificially, Naturally, Mystically Considered* [published in 1658 together with *Hydriotaphia Urne-Burial*],[11] Sir Thomas Browne (1605–1682) wrote what is probably the best-known English treatise on one aspect of numerology—specifically, the various significances of the number 5. (The book incidentally contains five chapters, as does its companion-piece. The total of ten chapters is not accidental.) Browne's sources included the body of medieval Jewish writing, based on the Old Testament, and known as the Cabbala, from which he took this illustration of 5 as a number signifying marriage resulting in generation:

The same number in the Hebrew mysteries and Cabalistical accounts was the character of Generation; declared by the letter *He*, the fifth in their alphabet; According to that Cabalisticall *Dogma*: If *Abram* had not had this Letter added unto his Name he had remained fruitlesse, and without the power of generation: Not onely because hereby the number of his Name attained two hundred fourty eight, the number of the affirmative precepts, but because as in created natures there is a male and female, so in divine and intelligent productions, the mother of Life and Fountain of souls in Cabalisticall Technology is called *Binah*; whose Seal and Character was *He*. So that being sterill before, he received the power of generation from that measure and mansion in the Archetype;

and was made conformable unto *Binah*. And upon such involved considerations, the ten of *Sarai* was exchanged into five.

Abram became Abraham and Sarai Sarah by processes which involved the letter *He*, the former by addition (Aleph Beth Resh Mem becoming Aleph Beth Resh He Mem), the latter by substitution (He for Yod). The change affected the situation in two ways, the lesser being that the number represented by Abraham's new name (248) was now identical with the total of the Affirmative Precepts,[12] and so fortunate and productive. More important, *He*, the fifth letter of the Hebrew alphabet, representing the number 5, was the seal and character of the archetypal feminine cosmic force, the generative *Binah*,[13] the mother of life and fountain of souls. When this was incorporated in the two names, the result was the promised birth of Isaac, although Abraham was then a hundred and Sarah ninety years old, an event which was cosmically significant because it marked the beginning of the chosen Hebrew people.

The letters of Eliezer's name produce a number: the best-known parallel in effect reverses the process. It is taken from the New Testament. Like the other New Testament writings, the last book, *Revelation*, is written in Greek, but in *13.18* the Number of the Beast is to be derived, in all probability, not from the Greek but the Hebrew alphabet.

'Here is wisdom. Let him that hath understanding count the number of the beast: for it is the number of a man; and his number is six hundred threescore and six.' The most probable solution is a Hebrew transliteration of the Greek name Neron Kaisar (Νέρων Καῖσαρ), Nero, the Roman emperor and persecutor of the Christians (37–68 AD)[14].

The method by which numbers are extracted from names, and *vice-versa*, stands in close relationship to gemetria, 'a cabbalistic method of interpreting the Hebrew Scriptures by interchanging words whose letters have the same numerical value when added' [OED]. This science, and the suggestion of magical practices which accompanied it, certainly affected some literary developments of numerology.

In early times, all this is to say, alphabetic and numerical symbolism tended to be closely related and to involve the super-natural or the metaphysical. In terms of literature, numerology may well be the child of alphabetic symbolism. Certainly the latter offers an approach to the history of the former.

The great fourteenth-century Irish manuscript, the *Leabhar Breac* [Speckled Book], contains a mixed Latin and Irish preface to St Columba's hymn, *Altus Prosator*, which among much else comments on the alphabetic order of the stanzas in the hymn, and the significance of some (not all) among the numerical features. The style of the comments is not original, nor even an example of insular eccentricity; the crucial one, for instance, on 22 as the number of letters in the Hebrew alphabet and of books in the Old Testament, derives from, or at least by way of, the Jewish priest and historian Josephus (37/8–c.105 AD), in his apologia for Judaism, preserved partly in the original Greek, partly in a later Latin translation, *Contra Apionem*[15] i.8. He contrasts the Jews with the Greeks, who possess myriads of books which are inconsistent and even self-contradictory.

Our books, those which are justly accredited, are but two and twenty, and contain the record of all time.

Of these, five are the books of Moses, comprising the laws and the traditional history from the birth of man down to the death of the lawgiver. This period falls only a little short of three thousand years. From the death of Moses until Arta-xerxes, who succeeded Xerxes as king of Persia, the prophets subsequent to Moses wrote the history of the events of their own time in thirteen books. The remaining four books contain hymns to God and precepts for the conduct of human life.

From Artaxerxes to our own time the complete history has been written, but has not been deemed worthy of equal credit with the earlier records, because of the failure of the exact succession of the prophets.

We have given practical proof of our reverence for our own

Scriptures. For, although such long ages have now passed, no one has ventured either to add, or to remove, or to alter a syllable; and it is an instinct with every Jew, from the day of his birth, to regard them as the decrees of God, to abide by them, and, if need be, cheerfully to die for them.

The five books of Moses are (1) *Genesis*, (2) *Exodus*, (3) *Leviticus*, (4) *Numbers*, (5) *Deuteronomy*. The thirteen books of the prophets subsequent to Moses are probably (6) *Joshua*, (7) *Judges* with *Ruth*, (8) *Samuel*, (9) *Kings*, (10) *Chronicles*, (11) *Ezra* with *Nehemiah*, (12) *Esther*, (13) *Job*, (14) *Isaiah*, (15) *Jeremiah* with *Lamentations*, (16) *Ezekiel*, (17) the Minor Prophets, (18) *Daniel*. The hymns and precepts are probably (19) *Psalms*, (20) *Song of Songs*, (21) *Proverbs*, (22) *Ecclesiastes*.

It is unlikely that the concept originated with Josephus; almost certainly we have here an echo of teaching in the rabbinical schools, which had passed into the full Christian tradition by the time of St Jerome (c.340–420). In the *Prologus Galeatus*[16] [Helmeted Prologue] to his new translation of the Bible into Latin, he wrote:

> Just as there are 22 elements [i.e. the letters of the Hebrew alphabet] by which in Hebrew we write everything we speak, and the range of human utterance is contained in the initial sound of the names which we give them, so there is a total of 22 books [in the Old Testament] by which, as if beginning with letters, the as yet tender and unweaned infancy of the just man is made wise in the doctrine of God.

Jerome goes on to list the books of the Old Testament in an order slightly different from that of Josephus. The parallel between alphabet, Old Testament and history, implicit in Josephus, is in Jerome made specific.

With such associations, 22 inevitably became a sign of universality, and was accordingly used as the groundplan of such varied works as the *City of God* of St Augustine (354–430) and the *De Rerum Naturis* of Hraban Maur (776–856), both in twenty-two books. In the New Testament it had already formed the basis of the cosmological *Revelation*, written in twenty-two chapters; in the Old, as Jerome noted, of *Lamentations*, several among the *Psalms*, and *Proverbs 31.10–31* (the famous ode in praise of the virtuous woman). In the Apocrypha it is to be found in the closing words of *Ecclesiasticus* [*51.13–30*]. Some of these will be discussed below.

With all this in mind, it should now be possible to make a sympathetic approach to the crucial section of the *Leabhar Breac* preface, which runs[17] thus:

There is alphabetic order in this hymn, in Hebrew fashion. So then the number of letters in the alphabet is the number of *capitula* [chapters, stanzas] in this hymn. The Hebrews, however, do not put their letters on the sides of their *capitula*, but each letter over its *capitulum* to the end of the hymn; and this is the reason for it, because the names of their letters have a meaning, and that meaning runs through the *capitula*. Further, to Hebrews, this is the cause of the sequence of the order of their alphabet, to wit, 22 letters in the Hebrew alphabet, for there are 22 books in the Old Testament. To Greeks, however, the reason of their having twenty-four letters is the ten senses of man and the ten commandments of the Law and the four Gospels. Whereas to Romans the reason for their having twenty-three letters is that there are ten senses of man also and ten commandments of the Law and the Trinity.

There are six lines in each *capitulum* save for the first *capitulum*, and sixteen syllables in each line, but seven lines in the first *capitulum*. Fitting it is to have six lines in the *capitula* in which mention is made of the creatures that were brought to completion in six days; but fitting for seven lines to be in the first *capitulum* for this reason, because it deals with God, because God is not on a par with his creatures, or it signifies the seven grades of the church, or because the number seven signifies totality, or it signifies the seven gifts of the Holy Ghost.

The author of the Preface, it will be seen, does not ignore the numerological features present in the poem, but instead tends to derive them from the fact that the stanzas are in alphabetic order,

a custom which he correctly identifies as Hebrew—Old Testa,
ment, that is to say—in origin. The Old Testament contains
several poems of this kind, known, somewhat confusingly in
view of the usual modern English meaning of the adjective, as
acrostic poems, the basic structure of which was familiar to
medieval scholars. Several of the *Psalms* are in this sense acrostic,
as in a more elaborate way are the five linked elegies which
together form *Lamentations* and commemorate the fall of Jeru,
salem in 586 BC. Of the acrostic psalms, the most familiar and
the longest is 119, 'the most formal and elaborate of them all', as
C. S. Lewis observed[18] in a brief analysis which brings out some
of the intellectual and aesthetic features of the form:

> The technique consists in taking a series of words which are
> all, for purposes of this poem, more or less synonyms (*word*,
> *statutes*, *commandments*, *testimonies* etc.), and ringing the
> changes on them through each of its eight,verse sections—
> which themselves correspond to the letters of the alphabet. . . .
> The order of the Divine Mind, embodied in the Divine Law,
> is beautiful. What should a man do but try to reproduce it, so
> far as possible, in his daily life?

So far as he goes, Lewis is right, but he does not fully bring
out the fact that the psalmist tries to reproduce the Divine Order,
not only in his life, but in the actual formal characteristics of his
art, his verse. The key words of the psalm are all aspects of utter,
ance, and correspondingly the psalm itself is built round the
basic elements of speech, the letters which represent the sounds,
which together make up the word and the sentence. The initial
word of each 8,verse section begins with the letter of the Hebrew
alphabet which corresponds to the position of the section in the
psalm as a whole; these letters, Aleph, Beth, Gimel, and so on,
are indicated in the text of the Authorized Version, although not
in the *New English Bible*.

Alphabetic order signals all the possibilities of utterance, the
completeness of discourse, even in *Lamentations*, where the
destruction of Jerusalem is presented as the last syllable of the
divine word which makes up an epoch in history. The form, a

sequence of 22, 22, 66, 22 and 22 stanzas [verses], with differing numbers of lines, is balanced and elaborate. The first and second elegies are arranged in three-line stanzas, the fourth in two-line stanzas: in all three every stanza begins with the appropriate letter of the Hebrew alphabet. The third has sixty-six single-line stanzas arranged in triplets, the lines of which begin *aaa, bbb*, etc. The fifth has twenty-two verses but no acrostic.

Nothing absolutely parallel is to be found in the New Testament, but at least one book, *Revelation*, shows that the traditions continued. The book turns on the phrase already quoted,[19] which in the first and last chapters John places in the mouth of Christ, 'I am Alpha and Omega, the beginning and the ending'. Alpha and Omega are, of course, the first and last letters of the Greek alphabet to which *Revelation* bears no structural correspondence. It is important, however, to notice that there is some correspondence with the Hebrew alphabet in that the book contains twenty-two chapters, and the Hebrew alphabet contains twenty-two letters. If we assume that for *Revelation* John adopted a pattern similar to that used by the poets of the 119th psalm and *Lamentations*, the significance is fairly easy to grasp. Form and content are closely related. The content is the complete history of the world, seen in the light of Christ's statement that he is the beginning and the ending. The twenty-two chapters, in which the history of the world finds formal expression, correspond to the twenty-two letters of the Hebrew alphabet, which in turn symbolises the total range of the Divine Utterance, which is also the history written by God in the book sealed with seven seals. Naturally enough in a work composed during the Domitianic persecution, the accent falls more on the last than on the first syllables of the utterance.

Many New Testament passages emphasise the Word as the organising power in Creation, from *Genesis*, 'And God *said* Let there be light: and there was light' [*1.3*], to St John's *Gospel*, 'In the beginning was the Word, and the Word was with God, and the Word was God' [*1.1*]. Equally, number is emphasised in many passages where precise terms of mensuration are applied to God in creation; *Isaiah 40.12*, for instance, where one finds 'Who has gauged the waters in the palm of his hand, or with its span set limits to the heavens? Who has held all the soil of earth in a bushel, or weighed the mountains on a balance and the hills on a pair of scales?'; *Job 38.4–7*, 'Where wast thou when I laid the foundations of the earth? declare, if thou hast understanding. Who hath laid the measures thereof, if thou knowest? or who hath stretched the line upon it? Whereupon are the foundations thereof fastened? or who laid the corner stone thereof; when the morning stars sang together, and all the sons of God shouted for joy?' The passage, however, most often cited by medieval and later writers is taken, not from these, or from the Old Testament proper, but from the late and apocryphal *Wisdom of Solomon*, a passage which must be read in context:

> For thy almighty hand, which created the world out of form‐ less matter, was not without other resources: it could have let loose upon them a host of bears or ravening lions or unknown ferocious monsters newly created, either breathing out blasts of fire, or roaring and belching smoke, or flashing terrible sparks like lightning from their eyes, with power not only to exterminate them by the wounds they inflicted, but by their mere appearance to kill them with fright. Even without these, a single breath would have sufficed to lay them low, with justice in pursuit and the breath of thy power to blow them away, but thou hast ordered all things by measure and number and weight. [*11.17–20*]

It is significant that the translators of *The New English Bible*, from which this version is taken, head chapters *10–12* 'Divine Wisdom in History'. Divine Wisdom, operating in the history which began with creation, has reconciled Love and Justice to produce a rational universe based on mathematical concord.

Wisdom of Solomon was probably composed at Alexandria during the first century AD; it is closer in time to the New than the Old Testament. In spirit, however, it remains akin to the latter, as may be demonstrated not only by the quotations from *Isaiah* and *Job*, but by the example of the acrostic *Psalms* and *Lamentations*, the literary structure of which deliberately embodies the principle of measure, number and weight. *Revelation*, in some ways the most traditional 'Old Testament' book of the New, continues the line of development, even under a new dispensation.

22 was thus only one of many biblical numbers invested with significance and structurally utilised. *Revelation*, for instance, combines with it the numbers 2, 3, 4, 7 (4 + 3) and 12 (4 × 3). The last pair are the most important. 7, in effect, represents time, 12 eternity, and 12 is most clearly significant in chapter 7, and its multiples, chapters *14* and *21*. Chapter 7 occupies the interval between the opening of the sixth and seventh seals, and describes the sealing of the servants of God in their foreheads. The sealing signifies the possession of eternal life while still living in time. There are 144,000, 12,000 from each of the twelve tribes of Israel—(4 × 3) × 1000 × (4 × 3)—listed in 4 verses [5 – 8], each containing 3 tribes. The 144,000 reappear at the beginning of chapter *14*, 'And I looked, and, lo, a Lamb stood on the mount Sion, and with him an hundred forty and four thousand, having his Father's name written in their foreheads' [*14.1*]. Chapter *21* deals with eternity itself, the cubical 12-fold structure of New Jerusalem: 12 gates, 3 on each of the 4 walls, each inscribed with the name of one of the 12 tribes: 12 foundations, each named for one of the 12 apostles: the 4 walls, each 12,000 furlongs in length and 144 (12 × 12) angelic cubits in height:

The length and the breadth and height of it are equal. [*21.16*] And the building of the wall of it was of jasper: and the city was pure gold, like unto clear glass. And the foundations of the wall of the city was garnished with all manner of precious stones. The first foundation was jasper; the second, sapphire; the third, a chalcedony; the fourth, an emerald; the fifth, sardonyx; the sixth, sardius; the seventh, chrysolite; the eighth, beryl; the ninth, a topaz; the tenth, a chrysoprasus; the eleventh, a jacinth; the twelfth, an amethyst. And the twelve gates were twelve pearls; every several gate was of one pearl: and the street of the city was pure gold, as it were transparent glass. [*21.19 – 21*]

Inside the city is the tree of life, 'which has twelve manner of fruits, and yielded her fruit every month' [22.2]. 12 is also found in chapter 12, where the woman clothed with the sun, travailing with a child who was to rule all nations with a rod of iron, has upon her head a crown of twelve stars. The child, clearly, is Christ. 12 increasingly dominates *Revelation* as it proceeds towards and beyond the consummation of time.

7, together with the other numbers, is most evident in the earlier chapters and during the struggle which produces the end of time. There are 7 letters to seven earthly churches; which occupy chapters 2 and 3. Of these 4 appear in chapter 2, 3 in chapter 3. 'The seven stars are the angels of the seven churches: and the seven candlesticks which thou sawest are the seven churches' [1.20]. After the ascent to heaven, which begins chapter 4, the greater part of the chapter is devoted to the four beasts round the throne of God. Chapter 6 tells how 6 of the seven seals are opened. The first four are the Four Horsemen of the Apocalypse; the latter two are preliminary to the opening of the seventh and final seal [chapter 8], which is the prelude to a whole series of 7's—7 angels with trumpets, 7 thunders, and 7 heads of the great red dragon, 7 golden vials full of the wrath of God. There is also a series of 7/2 (3½); the forty and two months (3½ years) during which the Gentiles shall tread under foot the holy city [11.2]: the thousand two hundred and three-score days (3½ years) during which the 2 witnesses will prophesy [11.3]; the 3½ days between their death and resurrection [11.9–11]; the thousand two hundred and threescore days spent in the wilderness by the woman clothed with the sun [12.6, 14], and the forty and two months during which the beast from the sea was allowed to speak great things and blasphemies [13.5].

This series of hints—it is no more—is enough perhaps to illustrate how complex numerical structure and reference in *Revelation* in fact is, and how closely it is related to the cosmo-logical history which it expounds.

Other biblical examples, less directly structural, though capable of development as structural elements, are, for instance, the twice seven years served by Jacob for Rebecca, the ten plagues of Egypt, the Ten Commandments, and such Pauline examples as 1 *Corinthians 13.13*, 'And now abideth faith, hope, charity, these three; but the greatest of these is charity', or *Galatians 4.22–9*:

> Abraham had two sons, the one by a bondmaid, the other by a freewoman. But he who was of the bondwoman was born after the flesh; but he of the freewoman was by promise. Which things are an allegory: for these are the two covenants; the one from the mount Sinai, which gendereth to bondage, which is Agar. For this Agar is mount Sinai in Arabia, and answereth to Jerusalem, which now is, and is in bondage with her children. But Jerusalem which is above is free, which is the mother of us all. For it is written, Rejoice thou barren that bearest not: break forth and cry, thou that travailest not: for the desolate hath many more children than she which hath an husband.
>
> Now we, brethren, as Isaac was, are the children of promise. But as he that was born after the flesh persecuted him that was born after the spirit, even so it is now.

In the Bible it is thus possible to find examples of numerological structure—the acrostic *Psalms, Lamentations, Revelation*—theoretical justification for the use of such a device, and a multitude of numbers which stand in close relation to some aspect of the divine creation. These were later elaborated and systematised. In his edition of Bede's *Historia Ecclesiastica Gentis Anglorum*[20], Plummer has an invaluable footnote[21] in which he lists some of the biblical numbers to which Bede, following Isidore and Arator, attached particular significance. 5, for instance, is the five books of Moses, or the law, the five senses, or the five ages of the world before Christ. 6 is perfection of work, because God made the world in six days. 7 is the Spirit and his seven-fold gifts, the sabbath and rest, penitence (because of the seven penitential psalms). 8 is the Resurrection on the eighth day of the week, which is also the first, and the day of Judgement, because it follows the seven days of the world's ages. It would be possible to continue the list almost indefinitely, and even so, Bede, or at least Plummer, misses 33, believed to represent the number of years in Christ's incarnation, and so a symbol of Christ himself.

Early medieval authors fully appreciated that the principles involved might be utilised to construct literary works of some complexity. In prose, for instance, we have the anonymous *Navigatio Sancti Brendani Abbatis*,[22] 'Voyage of St Brendan', which for so long enjoyed a reputation as the archetype of the tall story, and now has another, equally undeserved, as the narrative of a pre-Columban voyage of discovery to North America. It was probably composed in an Irish monastery during the tenth century.[23]

Plummer, in his *Vitae Sanctorum Hiberniae*,[24] printed a set of Latin verses which he entitled *De Sancto Brendano versus satirici*, 'Satirical Verses on Saint Brendan', and which concludes:

Ergo nugis his qui credit, notatur stulticie,
Quas qui scribit, et qui legit, tempus habet perdere.
Expediret magis fratrem psalmos Dauid scribere,
Vel pro suis atque fratrum culpis Deo psallere,
Quam scripturis tam impuris idiotas fallere
Ergo, frater, has fabellas decet igni tradere.   [45-50]

[The man, then, who believes these frivolities, gets a black mark for stupidity; anyone who copies or reads them, has time to waste. A brother would be better occupied transcribing the psalms of David, or singing them for his own sins and those of the brethren, than deceiving idiots with such unholy scriptures. Thus, brother, these silly tales should be put in the fire.]

Such a reaction stems from a total misconception, or rather from a failure even to attempt to conceive the narrative method and purpose of the *Navigatio*, which is basically allegorical and symbolic, with biblical numerology playing an important part. The author of the text twice makes use of the phrase *sacramentum rei*, 'the inward, spiritual meaning of the incident', in the course of the narrative. The first occurs in chapter *10*, where the mass for

Easter Day is celebrated for the first time on the back of the great
fish Jasconius, which Brendan's companions mistake for an
island. To Brendan himself, the *sacramentum* has already been
revealed in a dream. There is a clear enough relationship between
Jasconius, the symbol of time attempting to reach eternity by
joining his own head and tail, and the metaphor of the apostles,
especially St Peter, as 'fishers of men'—a metaphor which in
chapter 21 is given a different but parallel allegorical development. Also vividly present is the early Christian symbolism of
Christ himself as fish, represented by the Greek word ἰχθῦς,
'fish'. In chapter 12 the phrase *sacramentum rei* is used by Ailbe,
abbot of an otherwise silent, timeless community, to describe the
miraculous kindling of the altar lights, which are never con-
sumed. '*Spiritale lumen est*', he explains, 'It is a light of the spirit',
and compares it to the Old Testament miracle of the burning
bush, which remained unconsumed, and from which God
spoke to Moses.[25] This last was normally regarded as a type of
the unconsumed virginity of the Mother of God.[26]

There is a clear suggestion that the reader should no more
remain content with the outward form of events than did
Brendan himself when he prayed to God as *cognitor incognitorum
et revelator absconditorum omnium*, 'witness of the unwitnessed and
revealer of all hidden things'. *Depreor tuam majestatem*, he went
on, *ut mihi peccatori digneris per tuam magnam misericordiam revelare
tuum secretum*, 'I pray your majesty that you deign of your great
mercy to reveal your secret to me, a sinner'. Brendan's quest is for
the *terra repromissionis sanctorum*, which may perhaps be para-
phrased 'The Land of New Promise destined for the redeemed'.
Obviously the name contains a reference (slightly dismissive)
to the first, or Old Testament, Land of Promise, to attain which
Moses and the Israelites journeyed through the wilderness for
40 years, a journey which was interpreted as a type of Christ's
40-day fast in the wilderness, and so of the Christian fast during
the 40 days of Lent. The unit of 40 days, which is common in
the *Navigatio*, recalls all three, and shares with them overtones of
trial and preparation. In chapter 3, for instance, Brendan and his
community fast for 40 days in preparation for the voyage. In

chapter 6 they sail before a favourable wind for fifteen days, then drift for 40 days before they reach an island. In chapter 12 they are out of sight of land for 3 months, and are then forced to circle the island of the community of Ailbe for 40 days. In chapter 13 they leave the community of Ailbe, and continue their voyage until the beginning of Lent. Early in Lent they find the Island of the Well of Sleep. The south wind which eventually takes them from the Island drops after 3 days; they drift for 20 days, half of Lent, and eventually arrive at the island of their procurator (the Island of White Sheep) on Maundy Thursday, the commemoration of the institution of the Eucharist at the Last Supper. In chapter 16, after a 40-day voyage, they meet a sea-monster, which threatens to devour them. In chapter 18 they stay 40 days on the Island of Grapes. In chapter 27 the voyage from the Island of Paul the Hermit to that of the White Sheep occupies the whole of Lent. In chapter 28 they sail east with the procurator for 40 days before running into the mist which surrounds the *terra repro-missionis sanctorum*. Their stay in that land is for 40 days.

Typologically the voyage of Brendan and his companions thus corresponds to the journey of the Israelites through the wilderness. Even so, it must be said that the correspondence with Lent remains closer, and that throughout the narrative the recurrence of the number 3 tends to put 40 into a trinitarian and eucharistic—in other words a New Testament—context. 3 recalls Father, Son and Holy Ghost, and the 3 days inclusive during which Christ's body rested in the sepulchre. It is notice-able, however, that the association of 3, in terms especially of the 3 brethren who force themselves into the company of the voyagers, are by no means invariably trinitarian or eucharistic. Satan, it will be recollected, corrupted 1 in 3 of the heavenly host.[27] Both aspects of the number may be illustrated. In chapter 3, the 40-day fast is divided into 3-day periods (*ieiunium quadraginta dierum, semper per triduanas*), and Brendan spends 3 days and 3 nights with Enda. In chapter 5, 3 additional brethren join the company against the will of Brendan. These 3 govern the structure of chapter 6. The first fifteen days of their voyage, during which they receive a favourable wind, correspond to the original number of the company, to Brendan, that is to say, and his 14 chosen companions. For the next 40 days they drift until they see an island. For 3 days they attempt to find an anchorage, and when they are finally successful, they remain on the island for 3 days, during which the first of the 3 additional brethren is tempted by Satan in the form of an Ethiopian child and falls. The narrative implies that the original company would have found the island in 15 days, and that their subsequent difficulties are entirely due to the presence of 3 additional brethren. 6, the number of the chapter, is 3 × 2, and 2 is often, although by no means invariably, a number with evil associations.

In chapter *12*, when they leave the Paradise of Birds, they sail for 3 months before they reach the community of Ailbe, but, as has been mentioned, their landing is delayed for 40 days. The church on the island has 3 altars. In chapter *13*, after a long voyage, they sight an island at the beginning of Lent. At the time they have fasted for 3 days. The sea round the island is full of fish, which provide them with appropriate Lenten fare, but the water of the spring on the island is soporific. The brethren who drink 1 cup sleep for 1 day, those who drink 2 for 2, and those who drink 3 for 3. Only Brendan abstains. When they leave the island, they take supplies which will allow them to eat and drink every 3rd day during Lent. At the beginning of chapter *14* they have a favourable wind for 3 days. In chapter *16*, the sea-monster which threatens them is torn in 3 by the rival monster sent in answer to their prayers. 1 of the 3 fragments is washed up on the island they reach and provides them with food for their 3-month stay. In chapter *17*, they reach the Island of Anchorites where 3 companies, 1 of boys, 1 of youths and 1 of mature men, ceaselessly perform the Divine Office. The 2nd of the 3 additional brethren remains with the 2nd company. Chapter *18* includes 2 3-day fasts. There are 6 springs on the Island of Grapes.

Chapter *26*, which tells of the encounter with Paul the Hermit, is particularly full of 3's and multiples thereof. Brendan's company reach the island after a 3-day voyage. Paul has lived there for 90 (3 × 30) years, for 60 (3 × 20) of them without any corporeal sustenance, although during the previous 30 (3×10) an otter (*luter*) had brought him a fish every 3rd day (an effective piece of eucharistic symbolism). Paul's original voyage to the island took 7 days, 3 of directed navigation and 4 of drifting.

In chapter *28*, on the return voyage from the *terra repro-missionis sanctorum*, Brendan and his company stay in the Island of Delights, which belongs to Mernoc, their procurator, for 3 days and nights.

The Land of Old Testament Promise is firmly situated on earth. The Land of New Promise is different. It is Paradise, the New Jerusalem, which will be permanently revealed to believers only at the end of the world. *Post multa vero curricula temporum declarabitur ista terra successoribus uestris quando Christianorum super-venerit persecucio*, 'After many cycles of time, that land will be revealed to your successors when the persecution of Christians will have passed'. The last reference is to the final persecution of the Church as foretold in *Revelation*[28] and elsewhere.

To the extent that living human beings—Mernoc, Barinthus, Brendan and his companions—are able to win entrance, the *terra repromissionis Sanctorum* is the Earthly Paradise, the lost Garden of Eden, situated in some secluded portion of Earth to the east. But in its most important features it is, as I have said, the New Jerusalem. Christ is the light of the place, and there is no night. The fruit-trees remain in a perpetual autumn of ripeness, like those of the New Jerusalem which yielded their fruit every month. The river which bisects the island, and which living human beings are forbidden to cross, is the Water of Life, flowing from the throne of the Lamb, and dividing time from eternity. The revelation of the land is the millenium, the sabbath of rest, which is to follow the six ages of the world, just as the first sabbath followed the six days of creation.

7 is thus the number which typifies the *terra repromissionis sanctorum*, and the seven-year voyage of Brendan and his companions is an allegorical recapitulation of the spiritual history of the world. At its heart is the *sacramentum* of the eucharist in relation to the events of the Incarnation, a point emphasised still further by the four-fold division of the individual years which

make up the voyage. Each year, the period from Maundy Thursday to Holy Saturday is spent on the Island of White Sheep, types of the Paschal Lamb. The all-important celebration of the Resurrection during the Vigil of Easter Day and Easter Day itself to the sixth hour, is made on the back of Jasconius. The period of Easter Day to the octave of Pentecost is spent in the Paradise of Birds. Save in the seventh year, when they reach the *terra repromissionis sanctorum*, the period from Advent through Christmas to the octave of the Epiphany is spent with the community of Ailbe. The voyage thus contains 28 (4×7) fixed points, to which correspond the 28 chapters of the narrative as a whole, and it is perhaps worth noting that numerologically 28 as the second perfect (and therefore powerful and benevolent) number the factors of which $(1, 2, 4, 7, 14)$ themselves add up to a total of 28, is itself an appropriate symbol of the perfection of the *terra repromissionis sanctorum*. Although the Easter commemorations generally receive the greater emphasis, the *terra repromissionis sanctorum* is attained during the Christmas period, in anticipation, it may be, or as a type, of the Second Coming of Christ.

The 28 chapters themselves fall naturally into subgroups of 7. Chapter 7, the first narrative sabbath, tells of the final salvation and holy death of the first of the 3 intrusive brethren. The second sabbath, chapter *14*, tells of the second arrival at the Island of White Sheep for Maundy Thursday, Good Friday and Holy Saturday. The third, chapter *21*, tells of events one feast of St Peter (29th June), when as mass was celebrated, the ocean became transparent and they were able to see all the monsters of the deep *sicut greges iacentes in pascuis*, 'like flocks lying in pasture'. They are linked to the figure of the great fish Jasconius by the fact that they lie head to tail in a circle. The others ask Brendan to celebrate in silence because they are afraid that his voice may anger the sea-creatures. Brendan however sings in a louder voice than usual, and the sea-creatures assemble round the boat at a respectful distance to gaze on the Host. The symbolism is closely related to the figure of Peter, the fisherman who became a fisher of men.[29]

The fourth sabbath, chapter 28, sees the arrival at the *terra repromissionis sanctorum*, where the faithful are to spend the sabbath of the world.

14, the original number of Brendan's companions, means that the currach, in which they make the seven-year voyage, is appropriately propelled by 7 pairs of oars. The three brethren who force themselves into the company do not survive the voyage. 14 is also present as a multiple. When the company meets Paul the Hermit, he is 140 years old, and the great crystal column which in chapter 22 they find in the sea, and which it takes them 3 days to approach, measures 1400 cubits on each side. Like the New Jerusalem, it is a perfect cube.

7 also plays a part in the description of the community of Ailbe, in whose church there are 7 lights, three before the central altar, and two before each of the others. Like the altars, the church itself is square, and the combination of 4 walls and 7 lights once again hints at 28.

The 24 brethren of Ailbe's community, finally, correspond to the 24 hours of the day, and they are divided into two companies of 12, who celebrate the 6 canonical hours with the celebration of the eucharist taking place between terce and sext. The six canonical hours are related to the six days of creation and the six ages of the world; the eucharist corresponds to the sabbath. (The canonical hours are also observed in the Paradise of Birds, but as the birds are angels who fell, though against their own will, they do not celebrate the eucharist.) It is appropriately in chapter 12 that Ailbe's community of 2 × 12 is described.

The *Navigatio* survives in more than one hundred and twenty manuscripts, in addition to which several vernacular versions, which themselves attained considerable popularity, are known to exist.[30] Formally, it is a saint's *Life*, or rather the extended narrative of the episodes regarded as most significant in the legend of Brendan, object of a widely diffused cult extending into Europe from Ireland and the British Isles. The text of the *Navigatio* was often bodily incorporated into that of the more official *Life*, the *Vita Sancti Brendani Abbatis Clonfertensis*.[31] Brandon Bay and Brandon Mount in Co. Kerry, where the voyage is said to have begun, are still places of pilgrimage. The very attacks on the veracity of the *Navigatio* show how widespread and insidious its influence was felt to be. All this is to say that the numerologically constructed *Navigatio* had a very substantial medieval readership, among which only a few, no doubt, would appreciate the full complexity of its structure. Even the remainder, however, must have had some awareness of numerical symbolism, some inclination to accept it as contributing to the intellectual and emotional effect of the whole, and to expect its presence in other works of a broadly similar kind.

2

Plato. The Harmonic Soul of the Universe

The Republic—*Timaeus*—*Laws*—Cicero

```
  1 2 3 4
   5 6 7
    8 9
     0
```

The Navigatio Sancti Brendani Abbatis is, among much else, an example of the narrative form known as the Other World Journey, so familiar in many guises from Homer by way of Virgil to Dante, Spenser, Milton and the modern fantasists. From the earliest times it has been customary to incorporate numerological elements in such narratives—not infrequently elements derived from the system set out in a philosophical variation of the form, the myth of Er the Pamphylian, which forms a *coda* to the *Republic* of Plato (c.429–347 BC). I quote[1] the most relevant section, the account of the Spindle of Necessity. 'Necessity', ἀνάγκη, is, it will be recollected, elsewhere an important term in Platonic metaphysics—the 'errant' or 'irregular cause' (πλανωμένη αἰτία) of *Timaeus 48*—but it is uncertain how far in the *Republic* Necessity has acquired any such connotation:

> They came in four days to a spot whence they discerned extended from above throughout the heaven and the earth, a straight light like a pillar, most nearly resembling the rainbow, but brighter and purer. To this they came after going forward a day's journey, and they saw that at the middle of the light the extremities of its fastenings stretched from heaven; for this light was the girdle of the heavens like the undergirders of triremes, holding together in like manner the entire revolving vault. And from the extremities was stretched the spindle of Necessity, through which all the orbits turned. Its staff and its hook were made of adamant, and the whorl of these and other

26

kinds was commingled. And the nature of the whorl was this. Its shape was that of those in this world, but from his description we must conceive it to be as if in one great whorl, hollow and scooped out, there lay enclosed, right through, another like it, but smaller, fitting into it as boxes that fit into one another, and in like manner another—the third—and a fourth, and four others, for there were eight of the whorls in all, lying within one another, showing their rims as circles from above and forming the continuous back of a single whorl about the shaft, which was driven home through the middle of the eight. Now the first and outmost whorl [Fixed Stars] had the broadest circular rim, that of the sixth [Mercury] was second, and third was that of the fourth [Mars], and fourth was that of the eighth [Moon], fifth that of the seventh [Sun], sixth that of the fifth [Venus], seventh that of the third [Jupiter], eighth that of the second [Saturn]; and that of the greatest [Fixed Stars] was spangled, that of the seventh [Sun] brightest, that of the eighth [Moon] took its colour from the seventh [Sun] which shone upon it. The colours of the second [Saturn] and fifth [Venus] were like one another and more yellow than the two former. The third [Jupiter] had the whitest colour, and the fourth [Mars] was of a slightly ruddy hue; the sixth [Mercury] was second in whiteness. The staff turned as a whole in a circle with the same movement but within the whole as it revolved the seven inner circles revolved gently in the opposite direction to the whole, and of these seven the eighth [Moon] moved most swiftly, and next and together with one another the seventh sixth and fifth [Sun, Mercury, Venus]; and third in swiftness, as it appeared to them, moved the fourth [Mars] with returns upon itself, and fourth the third [Jupiter] and fifth the second [Saturn]. And the spindle turned on the knees of Necessity, and up above on each of the rims of the circles a Siren stood, borne around by its revolution and uttering one sound, one note, and from all the eight there was the concord of a single harmony. And there were other three who sat round about at equal intervals, each one on her throne, the Fates, daughters of Necessity, clad in white vest⁄

ments with filleted heads, Lachesis and Clotho and Atropos, who sang in unison with the music of the Sirens, Lachesis singing the things that were, Clotho the things that are, and Atropos the things that are to be. And Clotho with the touch of her right hand helped to turn the outer circumference of the spindle, pausing from time to time. Atropos with her left hand in like manner helped to turn the inner circles, and Lachesis alternately with either hand lent a hand to each.

The three Fates spin the thread of destiny on the spindle of the universe, which is also the spindle of Necessity, mother of the Fates; the whorl, which moves partly with, partly against, the spindle, is constituted by the celestial spheres inside the Milky Way. The image dominates the passage, details of which are to be interpreted, not as they provide a physical model of the universe, but mythically, in terms of the image. The relation of one part of the spindle to the other, that is to say, is governed not by physical reality, but by the image. The pillar of light is the Milky Way, the girdle of the heavens. The staff and hook, on which the thread of destiny forms, and by which the whorls are turned, has a similar role to play: in terms of later astronomical theory, it is the *Primum Mobile*, the outermost sphere by which the others are made to rotate in a single general direction, although Clotho, Lachesis and Atropos have the power to introduce minor significant perturbations, planetary movements, for instance, and the precession of the equinoxes. The whorl is formed by the eight inner celestial spheres. The rim of the outer-most and broadcast among them is, I suspect, the zodiacal belt, within which the seven planets appear to move; the range of their movements within the belt is indicated by the relative breadth of the rims of the inner whorls. The thread of destiny is twisted by the combined movements of the staff and that which the Fates impart to the different whorls—in other words, by the apparent movements of the heavens. Astrology, according to Plato, plays a part in the operation of destiny.

The order of the spheres differs from that usually found in classical and medieval astronomy; it follows the pattern known as Egyptian, because Plato was believed by later scholars to have derived it, by way of Philolaus (b.c.470 BC) and Pythagoras (fl.c.525 BC), from the Egyptian, Hermes Trismegistus.[2] Immediately above the planet closest to Earth, the Moon (8), is the sphere of the Sun (7), with Mercury (6) and Venus (5) next in ascending order. The usual order is (8), Moon; (7), Mercury; (6), Venus; (5), Sun, with the Sun central in relation to the seven planets as a group.

Long ago, W. A. Craigie, followed by J. Cook Wilson, noted[3] that a numerical principle underlay Plato's order of arrangement of the planets and zodiac in terms of breadth of rim, colour and velocity. The principle is that each of the three enumerations is

> based on combinations which rest on the number 9. A. If we write down . . . the numbers which express the orders of the whorls, and under each set the number which its rim has in the order of breadth, and then join those σφονδύλοι [whorls], whose united numbers produce a sum of 9, we have a symmetrical figure with its centre between the 4th and 5th, thus:
>
> Number of σφονδύλος   1 2 3 4 5 6 7 8.
> Order of width of rim   1 8 7 3 6 2 5 4.

B. Next, take the order of the colours. If we write down the numbers of the whorls in the order in which Plato mentions them when describing their colours we get:

$$1\ 7\ 8\ 2 \qquad 5\ 3\ 4\ 6$$

and there is here also a symmetry of arrangement with regard to the centre (and the centres of the two halves).

C. Finally, let us consider the order of velocities. The figure given by Cook Wilson is:

$$1\ 8 \qquad \begin{pmatrix} 7 \\ 6 \\ 5 \end{pmatrix} \qquad 4\ 3\ 2$$
$$=9 \qquad =9 \times 2 \qquad =9$$

In this figure, the order of velocities is observed; 'the group 1 + 8 (=9) is correlative to the group 4 + 3 + 2 (=9)', and the number 9 occurs twice in the central group, the members of which, being equal in respect of velocity, 'may be considered to have no order.'

It may also be noted that the order of velocities places positional and arithmetical emphasis on the Sun and its two immediate companions, Mercury and Venus, by assigning to them a sum (9 × 2) twice as great as that of either remaining group. From an earthly point of view, the Sun is obviously the most important planet, a point, as has been noted, which Plato does not emphasise in his account of the order of the spheres. He compensates however by his order of velocities.

As only eight spheres or whorls are mentioned, why should Plato have put such emphasis on 9? The whorls exclude the outermost sphere of the universe, the Primum Mobile as it was afterwards termed, here represented, as I have already suggested, jointly by the pillar of light (the Milky Way), to which the spindle is attached, and by the staff, which causes the whorls to rotate. Each of the eight Sirens, it will also be recollected, 'produced one sound, one note', but the eight notes together produced a 9th feature, 'the concord of a single harmony'. This in turn is taken up by the three Fates 'who sang in unison with the music of the Sirens'—not, that is to say, in unison with any single note, but with the concordant harmony. 3, in turn, is the square root of 9, or alternatively 9 is 3 squared. The spindle, finally, consists not merely of the eight whorls, but of these combined with the staff; in isolation from the staff the whorls have no function. 9 rather than 8 is thus the number which underlies the destinal structure of the universe.

Most important of all, perhaps, and linking the *Republic* with the later dialogue known as the *Timaeus*, to which the discussion now turns, is the 'concord of a single harmony', produced by the eight Sirens who stand on the rims of the revolving whorls. The relationship of the whorls is not, that is to say, merely numerical; it is harmonious in terms of the harmonic ratios established, it was believed, by Pythagoras. The figure of Timaeus, who speaks with such authority in the dialogue bearing

his name, appears to be based on a historical follower of Pythagoras, Timaeus of Locri Epizephyrii in southern Italy, the main
stronghold of the Pythagoreans. His words certainly are strongly
Pythagorean.

For Plato in the *Timaeus* the universe was a living creature,
an 'animal', vitalised by a soul, the Soul of the World or *Anima
Mundi*.[4]

The idea that the World-Soul must derive from numbers
and ratios was more apparently obvious to Greeks of the fifth and
fourth centuries B C than it is to the modern reader. So too was
the idea that these numbers and ratios must be related to the
mathematical harmony which is the 'soul' of music. The
mathematical basis of music is expressed by six arithmetical
ratios; *duple*, 2:1; *triple*, 3:1; *epitritus*, 4:3; *hemiolius*, 3:2;
quadruple, 4:1; *epogdous*, 9:8. The five corresponding consonant
musical intervals are the three basic, *diapason*, an octave, corresponding to *duple*, 2:1, *diapente*, a fifth, to *hemiolius*, 3:2, and
diatessaron, a fourth, corresponding to *epitritus*, 4:3, together with
bisdiapason, or double octave, corresponding to quadruple, 4:1,
and *diapente-and-diapason*, a double fifth, corresponding to triple,
3:1.

Soul for Plato was non-corporeal, and therefore abstract, but
more 'real' than the body which it vivified. As a consequence it
was closely related to the abstractions of number. At the same
time, it seemed obvious that if the universe was in fact animated
by a soul, its physical structure should demonstrably correspond
to its numerical basis. The substance of the soul Plato held to be
compounded of three abstracts, Existence, Sameness and Difference (οὐσία, τ'αὐτό, τὸ ἕτερον); this substance in turn was sub-
divided in terms of a three-part formula, the first part of
which runs thus:[5] God

(a) first marked off a section of the whole, and then another
twice the size of the first; next a third, half as much again as the
second and three times the first, a fourth twice the size of the
second, a fifth three times the third, a sixth eight times the first,
a seventh twenty-seven times the first.

This is usually and most easily interpreted in terms of the so-called Lambda Formula, the series 1, 2, 3, 4 (2^2), 9 (3^2), 8 (2^3) and 27 (3^3), arranged like a Greek capital lambda (Λ)

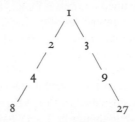

Plato does not limit his words however to single numerical series. Calcidius for instance, the fourth-century translator and commentator on the *Timaeus* whose work greatly influenced the Middle Ages and early Renaissance, based part at least of his commentary[6] on the parallel series 6, 12, 18, 24, 54, 48 and 162, and something of the kind is necessary if the later subtleties of the Platonic formula are to be understood. Plato himself introduced a ratio of 256:243 [$2^8:3^5$], which corresponds to the musical interval of a semitone.

The most straightforward interpretation, however, will serve for an introduction. The series is linked to the physical universe, first by the fact that it is made up of 7 integers separated by 6 intervals, corresponding, for instance, to the spheres of the seven planets, separated by the musical intervals, and so producing the music of the spheres, the seven phases of the moon, the seven-year periods of human life, and the seven orifices of the human head. Like the universe, the number 7 is self-generating and self-sustaining. The series, further, consists of the monad, representing the mathematical point; 2 and 3 which represent the one-dimensional straight line; 2^2 and 3^2, which represent two-dimensional surface; and 2^3 and 3^3, which represent three-dimensional volume. The abstract basis of the dimensions and properties of physical space is thus included. These and other important points are well-made in a work to which it will be necessary to return, the *Commentary* by the late fourth-century Neoplatonist, Macrobius, on the *Somnium Scipionis*:[7]

The fabrication of the World-Soul, as we may easily see, proceeded alternately: after the monad, which is both even and uneven, an even number was introduced, namely, two; then followed the first uneven number, three; fourth in order came the second even number, four; in the fifth place came the second uneven number, nine; in the sixth place, the third even number, eight; and in the seventh place the third uneven number, twenty-seven.

Since the uneven numbers are considered masculine and the even feminine, God willed that the Soul which was to give birth to the universe should be born from the even and the uneven, that is from the male and female. . . .

And then the soul had to be a combination of those numbers that alone possess mutual attraction since the Soul itself was to instil harmonious agreement in the whole world. Now two is double one and, as we have already explained, the octave (diapason) arises from the double; three is one and one-half times greater than two, and this combination produces the fifth (diapente), four is one and one-third times greater than three, and this combination produces the fourth (diatessaron); four is also four times as great as one, and from the quadruple ratio the double octave (bisdiapason) arises. Thus the World-Soul, which stirred the body of the universe to the motion that we now witness, must have been interwoven with those numbers which produce musical harmony in order to make harmonious the sounds which it instilled by its quickening impulse. It discovered the source of these sounds in the fabric of its own composition.

Perhaps by mere inadvertence Macrobius does not mention one interval already discussed, diapente-and-diapason, a double-fifth, corresponding to the ratio $3:1$, the triple, which is certainly present in the formula, and which is mentioned, for instance, by the much later poet, Robert Henryson (c.1420–c.1490).[8] More understandably, Macrobius makes no reference to the ratio $9:8$, the epogdous, at least partly because the corresponding interval, the tone, is dissonant. Plato, refers to it in the later and subordinate portion of his formula. The ratio appears to be present in the fifth and sixth integers of the primary formula, but this Plato, to judge by his subsequent elaborations, specifically excluded from the primary level; it is produced at a secondary stage of the process:[9]

(b) Next he [God] filled in the double and treble intervals by cutting off further sections and inserting them in the gaps, so that there were two mean terms in each interval, one exceeding one extreme and being exceeded by the other by the same fraction of the extremes [harmonic mean], the other exceeding and being exceeded by the same numerical amount [arithmetic mean]. These links produced intervals of 3:2 and 4:3 and 9:8 within the previous intervals, and he went on to fill all intervals of 4:3 with the interval 9:8.

It is to illustrate this part of the complete formula that Calcidius introduces[10] the series already mentioned, 6, 12, 18, 24, 54, 48 and 162: a series which fits the primary formula, but makes no provision for squares and cubes. Between 6 and 12 Calcidius insertst he two mean terms 8 and 9. 8 exceeds 6 by one-third of 6, 2; 12 correspondingly exceeds 8 by one-third of 12, 4. 9 exceeds 6 and is less than 12 by the same number, 3. 8:6 thus stands in the ratio 3:2 (hemiolius) and 12:9 is 4:3 (epitritus). The ratio of the two mean terms is obviously 9:8, epogdous. The integers of that part of the formula which is related to the basic 6 by the factor 2—12, 24 and 48—have mean terms, 16, and 18, 32 and 36, which follow the same pattern. Those related by the factor 3—18, 54 and 162—have mean terms 9 and 12, 27 and 36, 81 and 108, where the lower mean stands in hemiolius relationship to the lower extreme, and the upper mean in the same relationship to the upper extreme. The ratio 4:3 exists only in the means of the integers linked by the factor 2, and therefore, according to Calcidius, when Plato said that God filled all intervals of 4:3 with the interval 9:8, he was referring only to the series linked by the factor 2.

The octave corresponds to the interval diapason and the ratio duple, 2:1, but because the interval is also one which in musical terms includes 8 diatonic degrees, made up of five tones and two semitones, it is vitally related to the interval of a tone, epogdous. This forms the basis of the final sentences of the Platonic formula:[11]

(c) This left, as a remainder in each, an interval whose terms bore the numerical ratio of 256 to 243. And at that stage the mixture from which these sections were being cut was all used up.

Calcidius interprets this[12] in terms of the series 192, 216, 243, 256, 288, 324, 364½ and 384. The extremes of the series stand in the ratio 2:1—they represent, in other words, the first two integers of the initial Platonic formula (a), and represent the relationship of the octave, diapason or duple. In terms of (b), the means are 256 and 288. 256 exceeds 192 by 64, which is the third part of 192, and is less than 384 by 128, which is the third part of 384. 288 is midway between 192 and 384, and is separated from either by 96, which is half of 192 and one quarter of 384. 256:192 corresponds to 4:3, epitritus or diatessaron; 384:256 corresponds to 3:2, hemiolius or diapente. 288:192 corresponds to 3:2, hemiolius or diapente; 384:288 corresponds to 4:3, epitritus or diatessaron, and 288:256 corresponds to 9:8 epogdous or a tone. When the other integers are added to the series, four additional ratios—216:192, 243:216, 324:288 and 364½:324—are produced, and all are epogdous, thus creating five intervals of a tone within the series. The remaining two ratios, 256:243, mentioned by Plato, and 384:364½ are precisely equivalent (the quotient in both is 1.0534979), and represent an interval of a semitone. The two semitones complete the octave, and with it the musical structure of the Soul of the World.

The Platonic formula is common to the individual soul and the Soul of the World:[13]

So speaking, he [God] turned again to the same bowl in which he had mixed the Soul of the Universe, and poured into it what was left of the former ingredients, mixing them in much the same fashion as before, only not quite so pure, but in a second and third degree. And when he had compounded the whole, he divided it up into as many souls as there are stars, and allotted each to a star. . . . To ensure fair treatment for each at his hands, the first incarnation would be one and the same for all and each would be sown in its appropriate instru-ment of time [i.e. 'body'] and be born as the most god-fearing of living things. . . . After this necessary incarnation, their body would be subject to physical gain and loss, and they would all inevitably be endowed with the same faculty of sensation dependent on external stimulation, as well as with love and its mixture of pain and pleasure, and fear and anger with the accompanying feelings and their opposites; mastery of these would lead to a good life, subjection to them to a wicked life. And anyone who lived well for his appointed time would return home to his native star and live an appropri-ately happy life.

One should note, finally, the special importance in the *Timaeus* of 3 and its powers 9 and 27, an importance which obviously transcends that of 2 and its powers 4 and 8. (Both odd and even numbers were essential to Plato's scheme; not only did they represent male and female; all the basic ratios were either odd to even, even to odd, and a third possibility, even *or* odd to unity, which last was regarded as neither odd nor even.) 27 is in fact the sum of all the other numbers in the Lambda Formula $(1 + 2 + 3 + 4 + 9 + 8 = 27)$, and so in a sense contains them all.

Number for Plato is the reality which underlies every aspect of the universe of becoming; he was resolved, in J. N. Findlay's words,[14]

> to see in complex, many-dimensioned Numbers and Ratios, all transparently harking back to one or two ultimate Prin-ciples, the explanatory essence of everything—of Mind as much as of Matter, and of Value as much as Fact—the qualitative content of our experience being then regarded as a mere surface decoration on this numerical substructure.

Two further illustrations may be given. One is the mysterious Nuptial Number (or Numbers) which in the eighth book of the *Republic* is said to govern all cycles of existence. I quote the passage in what is perhaps the most uncompromising translation, that of Paul Shorey:[15]

> Now for divine begettings there is a period comprehended by a perfect number, and for mortal by the first in which augmentations dominating and dominated when they have attained to three distances and four limits of the assimilating and the dissimilating, the waxing and the waning, render all things conversable and commensurable with one another, whereof a basal four-thirds wedded to the pempad yields two harmonies at the third augmentation, the one the product of equal factors taken one hundred times, the other of equal length one way but oblong, one dimension of a hundred numbers determined by the rational diameters of the pempad lacking one in each case, or of the irrational lacking two; the other dimension of a hundred cubes of the triad. And this entire geometrical number is determinative of this thing, of better and inferior births. And when your guardians, missing this, bring together brides and bridegrooms unseasonably, the offspring will not be well-born or fortunate.

Findlay comments:[16]

The details of the Pythagorean passage need not be dwelt on here: Adam, in his great edition of the *Republic*, has perhaps given as satisfactory a treatment of them as can be given. Suffice it to say that they build on the charismatic properties of the right-angled, Pythagorean triangle, whose hypotenuse of 5, and sides of 4 and 3, very simply show that the square on the hypotenuse of a right-angled triangle is equal to the sum of the squares on its two sides. Multiplication, always a more fundamental procedure in the Pythagorean-Platonic philosophy than addition, yields 60 as the product of these three numbers, and sixty multiplied by itself thrice over (in due deference to the cubic solidity of such triple multiplication) yields 12,960,000, which can equally be regarded as a regular square number 3600^2 or as an irregular, 'oblong' number, the product of 4800 and 2700. The number 12,960,000 is approximately the number of days in a cycle of 3600 years, the Great Year of Pythagoras-Plato, the time it allegedly takes for all the planets to start together in a given stance towards one another, and to return to an identical stance. Making use of data in the later dialogue *Statesman*, the regular square number 3600^2 represents a period in the life of the cosmos when eidetic order and consequent uniformity ($\dot{o}\mu o\iota o\tau\dot{\eta}s$) prevails, when Units regularly mature into Lines, Lines systematically burgeon into regular Figures and Solids, and regular Solids into Solids regularly moving, and all into the completed patterns of organic life and life in society. The irregular oblong number 4800×2700 then arguably represents a subsequent period in which all this fine structure slowly disintegrates, in which $\dot{\alpha}\nu o\mu o\iota o\tau\dot{\eta}s$, non-uniformity, replaces uniformity, in which, in short, the blind, instantial forces prevail, and in which God, to use the language of the *Statesman*, has abandoned the tiller of the Universe, and has let Necessity rather than Mind direct. . . . The Great Year of the Universe, with its two cyclically recurrent variants, corresponds to two gestation periods in the life of the human embryo, the seven months period of roughly 210 days, and the nine months period of 270 days, and, as Adam puts it, the Great Year of the Universe may therefore be denoted by a rectangle whose sides are respectively the longer period and the sum of the longer and shorter period of gestation in the race of man, after it has been multiplied by the square of the Pythagorean perfect number 10. As the Universe is a *magnus homo*, and man a *brevis mundus*, these and similar analogies may well have seemed significant to the Pythagoreans, whom Plato is certainly copying here.

The second illustration to be given is the series of specifications for the new Cretan city, the institution of which forms the pretext for the greater part of Plato's latest certain dialogue, the *Laws*. Everything here begins from the number 5040, which not only is the product of the first seven integers [7!], but also possesses a total of no less than 59 factors:[17]

Let us assume—to take a convenient number—that we have five thousand and forty landholders, who can be armed to fight for their holdings, and that the territory and houses are likewise divided among the same number, so that there will be one man to one holding. Let this total be divided first by two, and then by three; in fact it will permit of division by four, five, and the successive integers up to ten. Of course anyone who is acting as a legislator must be at least familiar enough with figures to understand what number, or kind of number, will prove most useful in a given state. Accordingly we will select that which has the greatest number of immediately successive divisions. The whole integer series, of course, admits division by any number and with any quotient, while our five thousand and forty can be divided, for purposes of war, or to suit the engagements and combinations of peace, in the matter of taxes to be levied and public distributions to be made, into fifty-nine quotients and no more, ten of them, from unity onward, being successive. . . . The number of hearth fires established by our present division must remain for ever unchanged, without increase or deviation whatsoever. . . . Next, the founder must see that his city is placed as nearly as possible at the centre of the territory, after selecting a site possessed of the other favourable conditions for his purpose— it will not be difficult to discover or to state them. Then he must divide his city into twelve parts, but first he should establish and enclose a sanctuary of Hestia, Zeus and Athena —which he will call the citadel—from which he will draw his twelve divisions of the city and its whole territory. Equality of the twelve regions should be secured by making those of good soil small and those of worse soil larger. He should then make a division into five thousand and forty allotments. Each of these, again, should be bisected, and two half sections, a nearer and a remoter, paired together to form an allotment, one which is contiguous to the city with one on the border, one in the next degree of proximity to the city with one next most nearly on the border, and so on in all cases. We should further practice in these half sections the already-mentioned con-

trivance relative to the poverty or excellence of the soil and
effect an equalization by the greater or less size of the divisions.
Of course, the legislator must also divide the population into
twelve sections, constructing these sections so as to be as nearly
as possible on an equality in respect of their other property, of
the whole of which he will have made a careful record. Next
he will be at pains to assign the twelve divisions to twelve gods,
naming each section after the god to whom it has been allotted
and consecrated, and calling it a tribe. Further, the twelve
segments of the city must be made on the same lines as the
division of the territory in general, and each citizen must have
two houses, one nearer the centre of the state and the other
nearer the border. And this shall complete the business of
settlement. . . . Our immediate concern, now that we have
resolved on the division into twelve parts, must be precisely
to see in what conspicuous fashion these twelve parts, admit-
ting, as they do, such a multitude of further divisions, with the
subsequent groups which arise from them, down to the five
thousand and forty individuals—this will give us our brother-
hoods, wards, and parishes, as well as our divisions of battle
and columns of route, not to mention our currency and
measures of capacity, dry and liquid, and of weight—to see,
I say, how all these details must be legally determined so as to
fit in and harmonize with each other. There is a further fear
we must dismiss, apprehension of a possible reputation for
finicking pedantry if the law enacts that no utensil whatever
in the possession of a citizen shall be of other than the standard
size. The legislator must take it as a general principle that there
is a universal usefulness in the subdivisions and complications
of numbers, whether these complications are exhibited in pure
numbers, in lengths and depths, or again in musical notes and
motions, whether of rectilinear ascent and descent or of
revolution. All must be kept in view by the legislator in his
injunction to all citizens, never, so far as they can help it, to
rest short of this numerical standardization.

In his old age Plato is more pedantic, or perhaps simply more

disillusioned, than in his youth or middle years; there is nevertheless no mistaking the continuity between the *Laws* and the
earlier works. His general worship of number is summarised by
the Athenian, who continues to speak in *Epinomis*, an epilogue
to the *Laws*, which may be by Plato, or by his pupil, the
astronomer Philip of Opus. At worst, it is an early imitation,
consistent with much Platonic thought, and had considerable
influence on later cosmologies. The Athenian claims[18] that
ultimate wisdom is at least possible for man because Uranus, the
god of the eighth sphere, the starry heavens ($o\dot{v}\rho\alpha\nu\acute{o}s$), has given
him the gift of number:

> Well, and what god is it, Megillus and Clinias, of whom I
> speak in this solemn fashion? Why, Uranus, to be sure, whom
> it is our bounden duty to honour, as it is to honour all divinities
> and gods, and to whom we are specially bound to pray. All of
> us will confess that he is the source of all the other good things
> we enjoy, and we in particular assent that 'tis he who has in
> very deed given us number, and will renew the gift if men will
> only follow his leading. If a man will but come to the right
> contemplation of him, he may call him by the name of Cosmos,
> Olympus or Uranus as he pleases; only let him follow him in
> his course as he bespangles himself and wheels his stars
> through all their courses in the act of providing us all with
> seasons and daily food. Aye, and with the gift of the whole
> number series, so we shall assume, he gives us likewise the rest
> of understanding and all other good things. But this is the
> greatest boon of all, if a man will accept his gift of number and
> let his mind expatiate over the whole heavenly circuit.

This has the perfectly straightforward meaning that the
concept of number was derived from observation of the regular
movement of the heavenly bodies. In addition, it is implied that
number is the principle which finds expression in the movement
of the heavenly bodies, which as a consequence have the ability
to convey the idea of number to mortals here below.

The *Epinomis* with its doctrine of a living universe peopled by five orders of beings, corresponding to the elements of fire, aether, air, water and earth, was adopted almost wholesale by the Stoics, and influenced subsequent thought for many centuries. The *Timaeus* was even more directly powerful, especially through its effect on the philosophy of Cicero (106–43 BC) and his commentator Macrobius, and so eventually on the systems associated with the twelfth-century Chartres Platonists. By contrast, the *Republic* was scarcely more than a name to medieval scholars and poets. Cicero however wrote his own *Republic*, the *De Re Publica*,[19] the concluding portion of which, known as the *Somnium Scipionis* [Scipio's Dream], and corresponding to the myth of Er the Pamphylian, survived into the Middle Ages, accompanied, as we have seen, by the *Commentary* of Macrobius.[20]

Cicero's aim was to justify virtue in any earthly and temporal commonwealth by setting it in the context of everlasting realities. His basically Stoic philosophy is less abstract than Plato's, not so much concerned with the ideal Guardians of an ideal Republic, as with the qualities necessary if a statesman is to deal virtuously and at the same time effectively with the problems of communities in the Mediterranean world at the end of the Roman republican period. The career of the younger Scipio Africanus (185/4–129 BC) made him for Cicero the perfect historical exemplar, who in the *Somnium* sets out the plan of the universe in terms of which such a career finds its own justification.

Implicit in Cicero's text is a fair amount of numerology—in chapter II, for instance,[21] 'When your age has completed seven times eight recurring circuits of the sun, and the product of these two numbers, each of which is considered full for a different reason, has rounded out your destiny' (Scipio died when he was 56); in chapter IV,[22] 'The whole universe is comprised of nine circles, or rather spheres. The outermost of these is the celestial sphere, embracing all the rest, itself the supreme god, confining and containing all the other spheres' (The Uranus of *Epinomis*); in chapter V,[23] 'What is this great and pleasing sound that fills my ears?' 'That,' replied my grandfather, 'is a concord of tones separated by unequal but nevertheless carefully proportioned intervals, caused by the rapid motion of the spheres themselves,' and 'The other eight spheres, two of which move at the same speed, produce seven different tones, this number being, one might say, the key to the universe.' (The reference in this last is to the supposed fact that Mercury and Venus move at the same speed, and so produce the same tone. There are thus seven rather than eight tones—the five primary discussed by Plato, Macrobius seems to think,[24] together with superoctave, 9:8, and *leimma*, a semi-tone). Macrobius in his *Commentary* took every advantage of the opportunity for exposition afforded by these and other passages. One point he did not make. The subject of the *Somnium* is the 9 spheres of the universe; the text of the *Somnium* is divided into 9 chapters, which themselves might thus be taken as an elementary example of numerological composition.

Cicero's numerology is simpler than Plato's, and consequently easier to expound. Macrobius' *Commentary* was thus, generally speaking, more widely read, and so even more influential, than Calcidius's Latin *Commentary* on part of the *Timaeus*, which is more or less contemporary with the work of Macrobius and was known to the Middle Ages, but which is a formidable challenge to any but the most intellectually devoted and accomplished reader. The numerology of the *Timaeus* is not wholly compatible with that of the Platonic *Republic*; the system adopted by Cicero, however, made it possible to ignore the *Republic* and concentrate on the *Timaeus*. Macrobius includes material from the *Timaeus* in his *Commentary*. Chapter VI of Book I, for instance, the subject of which is the number 7 and its permutations, contains several references. The most important, even if in some ways the most difficult, comes at the beginning of the chapter:[25]

Hence Timaeus, in Plato's dialogue by the same name, says that the God who made the World-Soul intertwined odd and even in its make-up: that is, using the numbers two and three as a basis, he alternated the odd and even numbers from two to eight and from three to twenty-seven. The first cubes in either series arise from these: using the even numbers, two times two, or four, makes a surface, and two times two times two, or eight, makes a solid; again, using the odd numbers, thrice three or nine makes a surface, and three times three times three, or twenty-seven, the first cube. Accordingly we are given to understand that these two numbers, I mean seven and eight, which combine to make up the life-span of a consummate statesman, have alone been judged suitable for producing the World-Soul, for there can be no higher perfection than the Creator. This, too, must be kept in mind, that in affirming the dignity belonging to all numbers we showed that they were prior to surfaces, lines and all bodies; and besides we learnt a moment ago that numbers preceded the World-Soul, being interwoven in it, according to the majestic account in the *Timaeus*, which understood and expounded Nature herself. Hence the fact which wise men have not hesitated to proclaim is true, that the soul is a number moving itself.

The Lambda diagram underlies this passage and, as Macrobius points out elsewhere, it is made up of a group of 7 related odd and even numbers (or at least it was so interpreted—Plato's formulation, as I have mentioned, is deliberately more general and abstract). It is difficult however to see in what sense 7 and 8 have *alone* been judged suitable for producing the World-Soul.

Despite such occasional difficulties, the *Commentary* was enormously successful with Christian as well as pagan audiences. It was not difficult to find parallels in holy writ for much of the numerology. Christianity and Neoplatonism are not perhaps related in depth, but features in one possess attractive, if superficial, parallels in the other. Some—for example the rival doctrines of the Trinity—have numerological implications.

The main contribution of the classical world to numerological composition was thus theoretical rather than exemplary in a practical sense. Instances of composition in classical Greek or Latin are at best sporadic, in sharp contrast to the frequency with which abstract numerological relationships appear in cosmological theories on the border between philosophy and religion. Arithmetic had an almost mystic significance which in the modern world it has mostly lost, and one entire side of the educational system had as its basis this kind of arithmetic. The medieval student entered the *quadrivium*, the later stages of which were music, geometry and astronomy, by way of arithmetic. His textbooks derived from those written by Greek adherents of the Pythagorean and Platonic tradition, notably Nicomachus of Gerasa, who lived in the middle of the second century AD, and wrote *Introduction to Arithmetic* and *Theological Arithmetic*. In his study of Boethius,[26] Henry Chadwick comments:

> To Nicomachus Pythagoreanism is not simply a mathematic-ally based philosophy. It has the merit of offering a synthesis of science and religion, combining exact mathematical theory with a belief that the harmony apparent in the cosmos is the same that binds together soul and body in man. The four mathematical disciplines he calls *methodoi*, paths or methods for proceeding upwards in a steady progress towards higher knowledge. The standard Neopythagorean order is Arith-metic, Music, Geometry, Astronomy

The contents of such textbooks as these of Nicomachus were made available to the West in the encyclopaedic writings of such authors as Calcidius, Macrobius, Martianus Capella (fifth century AD), Cassiodorus (480–575), Isidore of Seville (c.560–636), and pre-eminently the philosopher and statesman Anicius Manlius Severinus Boethius (c.470–525), author of *De Arithmetica* and *De institutione musica*, as well as the great *De consolatione Philosophiae*. Chadwick remarks[27] that for Boethius, as for Nicomachus:

> the four mathematical sciences are a *quadrivium* [a word which Boethius apparently himself coined], a group of four ways by which, through the study of mathematical immutables, the mind may rise to the peak of perfection and learn to see the divine mathematics in creation. They are four progressive steps (*gradus*) liberating the eye of the soul (as Plato has put it) from corporeality. [Later he adds[28]] Outside the *Consolation*

of Philosophy no passage of Boethius has had a more potent
literary influence than the second chapter of the first book of
the *De institutione musica* where he distinguishes three kinds of
music: cosmic, human and instrumental.

All three build upon mathematical abstractions: the cosmic
holds together everything in the created universe; the human
blends incorporeal soul and physical body; the instrumental
alone resembles what is now generally understood by the term
music.

Boethius, as a curriculum author in schools of the ages
which succeeded his own, helped to shape the imaginations, as
well as the intellects, of the medieval and Renaissance writers who
produced the numerological compositions discussed in the next
three chapters. Behind him and his fellows stood the greater
figures of Plato and Pythagoras.

3

Node of Intersection. Celts and Carolingians

Augustine—Macrobius—Columba—Heiric—Hucbald

In the Old and New Testaments, as we have seen, numbers stand in close relationship to literary form as well as to the creative Word. In the Greek philosophical tradition of Plato and Pythagoras, numerical relationships pre-ordain the harmonic structure of the universe, but (at least to my knowledge) it is hard to find literary works which formally embody these relationships in their structure. In Latin literature of the classical period, the situation is moderately different;[1] but here, too, philosophic or other significance would appear not normally to have been conveyed by literary forms based on numerological relations.

The spread of Christianity among literate Hellenes and Romans made a considerable eventual difference, but initially led to no kind of merger between Hebrew numerological form and Platonic numerology. Some kind of philosophic merger is, of course, already apparent in the work of Philo Judaeus (c.30 BC–AD 50), in St John's *Gospel*, and in other writings of the 1st century AD. By the time of St Augustine the possibility of a formal merger had come much closer. His *City of God*,[2] for instance, resembles *Revelation* in the opposition which it postulates between Jerusalem and Babylon, the heavenly and the earthly city, and in its 22-book structure, corresponding to the 22 chapters of *Revelation*. At the same time it gives strong expression to Augustine's admiration of Plato and his followers —'we rank such thinkers above all others and acknowledge them as representing the closest approximation to our Christian position.'[3] Augustine in fact was steeped in Platonic philosophy,

47

sometimes to the discomfort of his later commentators. Almost the last point made by David Knowles,[4] for instance, in his discussion of the subject, is to condemn Augustine for his use of the Platonic hypotheses put forward in the *Timaeus* and elsewhere:

> Yet another strange Plotinian influence can be seen in Augustine's repeated inclination to toy with the Platonic and Neoplatonic conception of a World Soul, which in modern times has seemed not unattractive to Leibniz and even to Inge. Similarly, Augustine took from the Neoplatonists that interest in numbers, which to the ordinary reader of his works seems an idiosyncracy. We have seen that Plato, influenced by the Pythagoreans, tended towards the end of his life to see the ideal world—reality—as made up of mathematical concepts and symbols, which were therefore the metaphysical constituents of the visible universe. Plotinus adopted the conception, probably from the Neo-Pythagoreans, and Augustine in turn took it from the Neoplatonists. For him number is the intelligible formula which describes the qualities of being and the manner of change, so that all change throughout the universe, which presents so much philosophical difficulty, can in a sense be 'controlled' by numbers, just as an algebraic formula might express an electrical transformation or an engineering stress. Numbers are, in fact, a rationalization of the seminal reason of things. Numbers as used by Augustine had, of course, no scientific or mathematical basis, and it was easy, as Augustine found, to allegorize them, but the rational, or at least the pseudo-rational, foundation for what seems to many to be a strange aberration of a great genius can be seen to be one more legacy from Neoplatonism.

Knowles' own dislike of the Augustinian position has led him to underestimate the importance of the concept in Plato. The Augustinian way of handling numbers may be illustrated from *City of God* 11, chapter *30*, 'The perfection of the number six', and chapter *31*, 'The seventh day of completeness and rest', but in fact it is omnipresent in his work.

It is not surprising that Knowles extended[5] his distaste to include the works of Dionysius the pseudo-Areopagite, a Syrian monk, probably, of the early sixth century, who effectually concealed his identity under the name of St Paul's convert [*Acts 17.34*]. Again, Christianity and Neoplatonism merge in his works, the most important of which to the student of numerology are the *Celestial Hierarchy*, which explains how the nine orders of angels mediate God to man, and the *Ecclesiastical Hierarchy*,[6] which deals with the sacraments and the three 'ways' of spiritual life—purgation, illumination and union, explained as the three means by which human nature is deified. The Latin translation by John Scottus Eriugena[7] ensured that the works became as influential in western as in eastern Christendom.

No question of literary form arises with Dionysius. That of *The City of God* remains a simple transfer from Hebrew; the process is, in effect, no different from what is found in *Revelation*—Hebrew structure used in Greek or Latin to convey Hebrew ideas. Much the same is true of the early Latin Christian acrostics, the anonymous *Apparebit repentina dies magna Domini* [The great day of the Lord will appear suddenly], which Raby dates c.400,[8] and which deals with Judgement Day in terms of *Revelation* and Christ's prophecy in *Matthew 25.31–46*, or the slightly more familiar *A solis ortus cardine* [From the cardinal point of sunrise] by Caelius Sedulius, a hymn composed somewhere about 450, the subject of which is the earthly life of Alpha and Omega, Christ. (These are two only of many possible examples.)

Traces also remain of a pagan development, more in literary criticism than creation. The claim that the numerological author plays a part in his work analagous to that of God in the creation of the universe is perhaps implicit, but would not readily have been given public expression by a Hebrew or early Christian writer. Macrobius with his Neoplatonic education had no such reservations, at least in terms of the divine Virgil, whose poetry forms the main subject discussed in the *Saturnalia,* his longest extant work.[9] For him, 'there is a great similarity between the *divinum opus* and the *poeticum opus*; between the *deus opifex* and the *poeta*'.[10] I quote only one relatively insignificant detail from his other main piece of literary scholarship, already often men/tioned, the *Commentary* on Cicero's *Somnium Scipionis*:[11]

> All wise men admit that the soul was also derived from musical concords. Among these an important one is the diapason, which consists of two others, the fourth and the fifth. The interval of the fifth is based on the ratio of three to two and the interval of the fourth on the ratio of four to three; in one the first term is three and in the other four; this we shall discuss more fully in its proper place. Suffice it to say that the fourth and fifth are based upon these numbers. And from the fourth and fifth the concord of the diapason arises; whence Virgil, schooled in all of the arts, when he wished to express that men were fully blessed in all respects, called them 'O thrice and four times blest!'

This, admittedly, is a single, and indeed generally maladroit, comment on a single half/line (*Aeneid 1.94*), but it typifies the approach made by Macrobius to any literary work, whether in poetry or prose, provided only that it was by one of the 'ancients'— for him, preeminently Virgil or Cicero. Any number involved is likely to be of Platonic significance; numbers were used by these authors as they had originally been used by the Demiurge. An unexpressed corollary is that the work of any later author of comparable stature might make use of numbers in a similar way. So long, however, as a vital social distinction existed between Christian and Pagan, so long Platonic numerology failed to merge with biblical. Only when Virgil, Cicero, Plato were granted a kind of authority, in practical terms indistinguishable from that of David, Jeremiah and John the Divine, was such a merger possible.

That time came most quickly to Ireland, at least partly because Ireland had never formed part of the pagan Roman Empire, and so knew nothing of earlier conflicts between classical paganism and Christianity, Cicero and Christ, which had plagued more southerly regions. Irish paganism was almost totally different from classical, which arrived late and simul/

taneously with Christianity, and was received with almost equal veneration. The culmination of the process is the Christian-Platonic system of the universe devised during the ninth century by John Scottus Eriugena (c.810–c.877), an Irishman resident on the continent, who was a genuine Greek scholar, author of a subtle and original Neoplatonic interpretation of biblical material, laying special emphasis on creation as governed by abstract numbers and numerological relations: *Periphyseon*, still more often known as *De Divisione Naturae*.[12]

Eriugena, however, is the climax rather than the beginning of the process, traces of which may already be seen in *Altus Prosator*,[13] a cosmological, acrostic hymn, composed almost three centuries earlier by Columba, the saint of Iona, who lived from c.521–597. The *Leabhar Breac* Preface to this hymn has already[14] been quoted: now is perhaps the time to look at the actual text.

Altus Prosator, deals almost exclusively with the alpha and omega portions of world-history, with the Trinity, especially the Second Person, in creation, that is to say, and with the Second Person as Judge at the Second Coming. The work of Creation was completed by the re-establishment of the natural order after the Flood. Except in so far as it is made clear that the Second Coming is a return, the First Coming, God in Incarnation, is virtually ignored, as is the entire sequence of events separating Flood from Judgement. History is seen in terms of six World Ages, corresponding to the six days of Creation; the first from Adam to Noah (the Flood), the second from Noah to Abraham, the third from Abraham to David, the fourth from David to Daniel, the fifth from Daniel to John the Baptist (the Incarnation), the sixth from John to Judgement and the end of the world. This last is to be followed by the seventh age, the Sabbath of Eternity.

The first ten stanzas, which form the alpha section, bring events down to the Flood. The A stanza is concerned with the Trinity apart from Creation: B with the creation of the angelic orders: C and D with the unsuccessful rebellion of Lucifer: E with the creation of the material universe and of man: F with the beginning of time, marked by angelic praise for the work of creation: G and H with the second fall of Lucifer, caused by the seduction of Adam and Eve: I and K (J is omitted as a mere variant of I) with the Flood and the subsequent re-establishment of an order which still survives.

The next five stanzas (L to P) deal with the main features of order established after the Flood. L is concerned with the waters which no longer overwhelm the earth: M with the globe of the world poised on the abyss: N and O with Hell, the lowest realm of creation, and P with the Earthly Paradise from which Adam and Eve were expelled after their seduction but which survives in a remote part of the world. Everything under the moon finds a place.

The omega section occupies the eight final stanzas. Q treats the appearance of God to Moses on Mount Sinai [*Exodus 12, 16–21*] as a type of the coming of Christ in Judgement. R, S and T deal with the Day of Judgement and the Resurrection of the Dead, V (U and W are omitted as mere variants of V) deals with astronomical types of the Second Coming, which in X marks the end of time, when the stars fall from their spheres and the material universe is destroyed. Y deals with Heaven as described in *Revelation 4*: Z with the final destruction of the adversaries of Christ, and the eternal union with him of the faithful.

To this very substantial degree form and content are biblical, but much of the detailed structure is Neoplatonic, derived quite possibly primarily from Macrobius. Thus the alpha section contains ten stanzas, and 10, the decad, is the first limit of numbers appropriate to the first age of history. The material creation begins at the mid-point of this section, the fifth (E) stanza, where the work of the 6 days is listed in the order found in *Genesis*. 6 is obviously important for this part of the poem; the first 6 stanzas (A–F) cover the entire creative process from the Trinity through the angels to the natural world of man; in F, the 6th stanza, the song of the angels, which is to be equated with the music of the spheres caused by the movements of stars and planets, marks the beginning of time, the passage of which distinguishes the lower from the upper creation. In B, 6 of the nine orders of angels are listed with the implication that these—Angels, Archangels,

Principalities, Thrones, Powers and Virtues—are the orders particularly involved with the six days' work, while the unlisted 3—Cherubim, Seraphim and Dominations—subsist in immedi-ate attendance on the Trinity.

In terms of biblical numerology, it is perhaps slightly surprising that the six days should themselves be described in the 5th stanza. One reason has already been given, and others may be advanced with some plausibility. No only is the 5th stanza the mid, and therefore most significant, point of the alpha sequence, 5 as a number possesses certain qualities relevant to this stage of the poem:[15]

> It alone embraces all things that are and seem to be. . . . This number designates at once all things in the higher and lower realms. There is the Supreme God; then Mind sprung from him, in which the patterns of things are contained; there is the World-Soul, which is the fount of all souls; there are the celestial realms extending down to us; and last, the terrestrial realm; thus the number five marks the sum total of the universe.

The Columban universe differs in detail from the Neoplatonic; the five-fold hierarchy in *Altus Prosator* is Father, Son, Spirit, Angels, Lower Creatures; but beyond doubt the totality of the spiritual and material universe is included in the first five stanzas, and the creation of the material universe is delayed to the fifth.

The next section, L–P, consists of five stanzas, and the points just made remain valid. On the level of the sublunary world, the stanzas embrace all things that are and seem to be. They deal with the main features of that world as God established it after the Flood, and as it exists at present. The lower creation is also the region of the five 'ports of knowledge',[16] the external senses; the constituent elements may be seen, heard, touched, tasted or smelled. The five stanzas, finally, represent the five ages from Flood to Judgement during which the postdiluvian order will endure.

8, the number of stanzas in the omega section, Q–Z, also has special properties. The central subject-matter here is the Last

Judgement, the final Court Of Justice, and:

> The Pythagoreans, indeed, called the number eight Justice
> because it is the first number that may be divided into two
> equal even numbers and divided again into two more equal
> even numbers. It is also the product of equals: two times two
> times two. Since it is the product of equal even numbers and
> may be divided equally, even down to the unit, which does
> not admit of division in mathematical computation, it deserves
> to receive the name Justice.[17]

The Last Judgement also marks the establishment of the New
Jerusalem, the bride of the Lamb, the Church Triumphant,
which John saw 'coming down from God out of heaven', and
which 'lieth foursquare, and the length is as large as the breadth:
and he measured the city with the reed, twelve thousand
furlongs. The length and the breadth and the height of it are
equal' [*Revelation 21, 2: 16*]. New Jerusalem, each side of which
had a length of some fifteen hundred miles, dwarfs its prototype,
the cubical Holy of Holies in Solomon's temple [*I Kings 6,20*],
but what matters is not the order of magnitude, but the figure of
the cube, symbolizing fullness, completion, consummation.
Here too Macrobius is relevant. Eight (2^3) is the first cube:

> Hence it is apparent that the number eight both is and is con-
> sidered a solid body, if indeed one is represented by a point, two
> by the drawing of a line (which, as we said above, is limited
> by two points) and four by points arranged at right angles to
> each other, with lines extending between the points to form a
> square. When these four are duplicated and made eight,
> forming two equal squares, and one is superimposed upon the
> other, giving the figure altitude, the result is a cubical figure,
> which is a solid body.[18]

The eight stanzas represent the cubical New Jerusalem.

The movement of the entire poem, finally corresponds to the
Neoplatonic concept of descent and reascent, emanation and
return, as the process of creation. The A stanza depicts the
Trinity as it has existed from eternity: the Z stanza depicts the

reabsorption into its source of the redeemed intellectual creation.

The Neoplatonic element, though certainly present, is decidedly subordinate to the biblical. In this respect *Altus Prosator* is the ancestor of *Navigatio Sancti Brendani Abbatis,* in which, as has been shown, the numerology is biblical to an even greater extent, although even here (as has been noted) 28 is strongly emphasised, presumably as the second perfect number, the factors of which (1, 2, 4, 7, 14), when added together make up the original number. Such numbers gain symbolic value by this excessive rarity: between 1 and 40,000,000 only seven (6: 28: 496: 8128: 130,816: 2,096,128: 33,550,336) are to be found, in which, it will be noted, the final digit alternates between 6, the first perfect number, and 8, the final digit of 28, the second perfect number. A 'perfect' number stands appropriately for the *terra repromissionis sanctorum* the perfect land reserved for the redeemed at the end of the world. The concept of a perfect number is Platonic rather than biblical.

Save perhaps in scale, and in its Platonism, *Altus Prosator* is not unique among early Irish Latin compositions. Other poems in the *Liber Hymnorum* are acrostics.[19] Numerological composition was familiar to a number of Columba's near contemporaries. *The Antiphonary of Bangor*[20] is a collection of prayers, canticles and hymns compiled between 680 and 691 at the monastery of Bangor in Co. Down, and now preserved in the Ambrosian Library at Milan, to which it was brought by Cardinal Federico Borromeo (1564–1631), the founder of the library, from Bobbio, founded by Columbanus (c.550–615), a disciple and fellow-countryman of Comgall (c.516–602), first abbot of Bangor. A later disciple of Columbanus no doubt originally brought the collection to Bobbio. The contents of the *Antiphonary* were intended to be sung or chanted (as indeed was *Altus Prosator* and the other contents of *Liber Hymnorum*. All these compositions were written with musical performance in mind).

One of the earliest hymns which it contains, *Sancti, venite, Christi corpus sumite*[21] ('Come, saints, take the body of Christ' more familiar perhaps in J.M. Neale's translation 'Draw nigh,

and take the Body of the Lord'), intended for use at the communion of priests, has a numerological basis. As usually printed,
it is 44 short lines in length. The short lines (alternate iambic
penthemimer and trochaic dimeter catalectic) are better, however, regarded as half-lines. The whole is then 22 lines, concluding with the significant couplet:

Alpha et ω ipse Christus Dominus
venit, venturus iudicare homines

[Alpha and Omega, Christ himself, the Lord, comes, who
will come to judge men.]

Although it is much briefer, the hymn clearly belongs to the
same tradition as *Altus Prosator,* and may be as old as the fifth
century. According to the rubric, it was sung by angels at mass
when St Patrick (c.389–c.461) and St Sechnall (?ob.447)
were reconciled after a quarrel. It was also regarded as having
11 2-line stanzas because 11 of the apostles present at the institution of the eucharist received the sacrament worthily.

Benchuir bona regula [Bangor of the good monastic rule], a
seventh-century panegyric of the monastery, also preserved in the
Antiphonary,[22] may be regarded as consisting of 20 lines or 40
half-lines. Both numbers are significant. Stanza six describes
the monastery in terms of the biblical Ark of the Covenant, said
to contain the two tablets of stone given to Moses on Mount
Sinai, carried by four Israelites in their 40-year sojourn in the
wilderness, and eventually housed in the Holy of Holies of
Solomon's Temple. This last was built as a cube 20 cubits on
each side and in height. It was overlaid with pure gold, while the
ark itself was overshadowed by two gigantic images of cherubin
whose wings touched (*I Kings, 6.16ff*). All these details are
present in the stanza, but applied to the monastery at Bangor:

Arca Cherubin tecta, omni parte aurata,
sacrosanctis referta, viris quattuor portata

[Ark protected by Cherubin, covered with gold on all sides,
full of sacrosanctities, carried by four men.]

The 'sacrosanctities' are primarily the tablets of stone, metaphorically the monks; the 'four men' are probably the abbot and his three most senior colleagues.

20, and 40 are thus both implicit in the stanza, as in stanza four is the 40-year journey in the wilderness:

Domus deliciis plena, super petram constructa,
necnon vinea vera ex Aegypto transducta

[A house full of joys, founded on the rock, and also the true vine brought out of Egypt.]

The second line combines a reference to *Exodus* with one to *Psalm 80.8,* 'Thou hast brought a vine out of Egypt: thou hast cast out the heathen, and planted it'. Stanza three, in turn, carries a reference to the 40 days and nights of rain which caused the Flood, on which Noah's Ark floated:

Navis nunquam turbata, quamvis fluctibus tonsa,
nuptiis quoque parata regi Domino sponsa.

[A ship never tossed, though clipped by the waves, a spouse also prepared for marriage to the king, her Lord.]

In the last two quotations, the Old Testament images, with their numerical references, are combined in resolved paradox with the New Testament images of the House built upon Rock [*Matthew 7.24-5*] and the Bride of the Lamb [*Revelation 21.9ff*]. The Bride is also, it will be recollected, simultaneously the cubical New Jerusalem, of which the Old Testament type was Solomon's Holy of Holies. The combination of numerological structure and imagery gives much of its power to this fine poem.

The *Navigatio Sancti Brendani Abbatis,* as has been noted, is another Irish numerological work of the later Carolingian period. Carolingian works of slightly earlier date show in their numerology a strong Platonic influence, mediated probably by the teaching and writing of the Irishman already mentioned, John Scottus Eriugena. During the reign of Charlemagne's scholarly grandson, Charles the Bald (823-877), it became familiar literary practice for Latin poets to combine Christian subject matter, a more or less classical style and versification, and numerological composition on a Platonic basis. Of these compositions, the best, perhaps, is the metrical *Life of Germanus*, saint and bishop of Auxerre (c.378–448), a *Life* composed towards the end of Charles' reign by Heiric[23] (c.840–c.876), a monk of Auxerre. Heiric was a famous teacher of arithmetic and computation, and the structure of his poem is based on the number 6. Curtius remarks:[24]

> It was an original thought of Heiric of Auxerre to base the elaborate structure of his life of St Germanus on this number. The work is prefaced by a metrical prayer of 19 6-line stanzas. An *Allocutio ad librum* in 72 ($= 6 \times 12$) lines follows. The work itself is divided into six books. The verse *praefationes* of Books II–VI have 48, 32, 48, 70 lines. The *praefatio* to Book VI begins with a eulogy of the number 6, then discusses other theological symbolic numbers.

The final sentence does less than justice to the *praefatio* to Book VI, perhaps the single most important early-medieval statement in verse of some aspects of numerology in relation to the narrative structure of poetry. The poem is too long to quote here in the original semi-macaronic form: it is written in Latin, interspersed with Greek words and phrases, derived apparently from glossaries rather than any real acquaintance with the Greek tongue. The style and vocabulary is generally Neoplatonic, for which the most immediate source is the work of Heiric's older contemporary, Scottus Eriugena.

The metre of the *praefatio* is itself significant; the couplets in which it is written consist of a dactylic hexameter followed by a penthemimer, the two and one half metrical feet which in the hexameter precede the caesura—in effect, a half-hexameter. The basic hexameter contains, of course, *six* feet, while the word penthemimer also contains a numerical reference, to the five half-feet which constitute the metrical unit. The metre is thus particularly appropriate to a poem on six and its relation to other numbers.

The *praefatio* may be translated as follows:

As you see, kind reader, the most beautiful Hexad brings this poem to an end. If you ask why, and what allegorical meanings are involved, it will not take me long to explain.

When the Creator began to fashion the universe, he based his plan on the enduring qualities of the Hexad. Although it is a truth expounded by theology that in the divine mind everything was created simultaneously by a single operation, yet, as the sacred page shows, God used this same number to determine all his work. The perfection of the number, conformable in all its parts, indicates the perfection of the work when it was completed. If you make an analysis of the numbers from one to ten, those of the first division, you will find that six is the most distinguished, for it is the only one which consciously forces itself to keep due measure within its own bounds, nor, when it is factorized, does it fall beneath, or wish to exceed, the sum of its factors. One is one-sixth, two one-third, three one-half; these factors together re-establish six $(1/6 + 1/3 + \frac{1}{2} = 1 : 1 + 2 + 3 = 6)$.

Reader, do you want me to relate something at which you will marvel still more? Come hither, ponder it. If the factors are set out in appropriate order, the entire Decad issues from the Hexad. One-sixth is the Monad, the first progression of number; it advances in first position. One-third, the Dyad holds its place as second; it is the source of equality. In third position is placed one-half, the Triad, from which inequality flows. The middle, the Triad, is added to the sixth, the Monad, and hence flows the genial Tetrad. One-third the Dyad, joins together with middle, the Triad; from these the Pentad takes its origin. The factors poured out in totality, as providence has allotted them, form the Hexad. The whole joined with one-sixth brings forth the dutiful Heptad, who is, they say, a virgin. One-third with the whole creates the Ogdoad; hence flows the hope that we shall live beyond our ashes. The whole with the middle numerologically begets the Ennead; it triples the Triad. If the Monad is added to these, it produces the Decad, the consummation of every number. So will the merits of this work win the eternal reward signified by the Decad. This remains as true as the sun which is above everything, nor does Reason falter.

Reader, surely you would not say that I had failed to bring out the full significance of the Hexad? Produce, if you can, another number renowned for the same arithmetical properties; let the Hexad then yield place. But if this is impossible, learn that the triumph of perfection contained in the number is appropriate to my patron, Bishop Germanus, whom you would correctly describe as a fellow-labourer with God.

Whatever work remains, you will speed it better by a modest prayer. O merciful Trinity, you are also source of our individual trinities, for every thing lies concealed in three. Philosophers talk, for instance, about Essence, Power and Action, without which Nature could not exist. There is also a trinity co-terminous with the human soul, by virtue of which it becomes the image of God; the constituents here are Mind, Word, and Discursive Thought; Thou bestowest this also. Come then, Supreme God, Trinity, grant the attainment of the desired goals. For fear that despite everything weariness should oppress the exhausted mind, we proceed under thy leadership.

The basis for this is a combination of ideas derived from the *Timaeus* and the first chapter of *Genesis*. Plato provided the concept that creation was the embodiment of a plan which existed eternally in the mind of the Demiurge, the Creator:[25]

It (the universe) must have been constructed on the pattern of what is apprehensible by reason and understanding and eternally unchanging; from which again it follows that the world is the likeness of something else. . . . God's purpose was to use as his model the highest and most completely perfect of intelligible things.

The plan, the pattern, the model, as eternal, itself stood outside time:

For before the heavens came into being there were no days or nights or months or years, but he devised and brought them into being at the same time that the heavens were put together. The creation of the Soul of the Universe had an abstract six-fold basis, the constituents of which were (1) Indivisible Existence (2) Divisible Existence (3) Indivisible Sameness (3) Divisible Sameness (5) Indivisible Difference (6) Divisible Difference. These on the first mixture gave rise to the triad of Intermediate Existence, Intermediate Sameness and Intermediate Difference, which on the second mixture produced the monadic Soul. This six-fold basis provided a link with the six days of creation in *Genesis*, and so produced a numerological reconciliation of Platonic with Christian thought, confirmed by the fact that 6 was itself a perfect and, in combination with its factors, a generative number.

The orderly derivation of all other numbers (primarily, but not only, those of the first decad) from 6 and its factors, confirms that 6 is unique. The properties attributed to the individual numbers usually have some kind of Platonic origin; the description, for instance, of the Tetrad as 'genial' (*alma τετρας*) derives from the fact, noted by Plato, Macrobius and others that 4 is the first number to possess two means, 2 and 3, between itself and unity. In terms of the four constituent elements—earth, water, fire and air of the pre-seventeenth-century lower universe—this fact has considerable cosmological implications.

Borrowing the means from this number the creator of the universe bound the elements together with an unbreakable chain, as was affirmed in Plato's *Timaeus*: in no other way could the elements earth and fire, so opposed and repugnant to each other and spurning any communion of their natures, be mingled together and joined in so binding a union unless they were held together by the two means of air and water. For thus, in spite of the utter diversity of these elements, the Creator harmonized them so skilfully that they could be readily united.[26]

The harmony, in other words, of the four elements is derived from the harmonic, 'genial' properties of the number 4.

From at least the time of Pythagoras, the properties of the

heptad 7 caused it to be regarded as numerologically the equivalent of the twice-virgin goddess, Pallas Athene. She, it will be remembered, had no mother but sprang fully-armed from the head of her father, Zeus, and led her immortal existence in virginity. Like Pallas, 7 is not begotten; as a prime number, that is to say, it springs fully-armed from the head of its parent, the monad. As a factor, it does not yield a number within the decad, and so does not beget. No other number in the decad possesses this combination of qualities. In biblical terms it corresponds to the seventh day, the sabbath, and to the Virgin, born of an Immaculate Conception, and herself the vessel of a virgin birth. Seven sorrows and seven joys are particularly associated with the Christian Virgin.

The heptad is called 'dutiful' (*officiosam*) because so many functions are ascribed to it in Neoplatonic writings. Macrobius, for instance, considers both eight and seven to be 'full' numbers, to each of which he devotes a chapter of his *Commentary*. That devoted to eight, chapter v of Book I,[27] contains eighteen sections. That devoted to seven, chapter VI,[28] contains eighty-three sections, and concludes with obvious justice, 'The number seven is distinguished for having so many functions, whether exercised in the combinations amounting to seven or by itself, that it is deservedly considered and called full'. From 'full' to 'dutiful' is no more than a step.

The ogdoad gives rise to the hope that we shall live beyond our ashes because 8 represents the celestial regions, the eighth sphere, beyond the prison-house of the seven planets—Moon, Sun, Mercury, Venus, Mars, Jupiter and Saturn—postulated by pre-Copernican astronomy as the home of mortal endeavour. The developed concept of the ogdoadic region is Gnostic[29] rather than Platonic, but it ultimately derives from the Plain of Truth beyond the heavens described in Plato's *Phaedrus*,[30] while an intermediate stage is the concept of the descent and return of souls through the seven planetary spheres, briefly expounded by Macrobius in Book I, chapter *12* of his *Commentary*.[31]

Apart from the metrics, all these points are matters of inter-pretation rather than structural analysis, but Heiric's prologue may itself have a basis in numerology. St Germanus lived the biblical span of seventy years; the prologue to the book which completes his *Life* correspondingly occupies 70 lines. It may be coincidence, but nevertheless should be noted, that within the prologue Heiric's demonstration that all other numbers derive from six and its factors occupies 28 lines, and that 28 is the second perfect number, with factors, 14, 7, 4, 2 and 1, themselves totalling 28. In addition, 28 is the sum of the monad and the first six true numbers, 2, 3, 4, 5, 6, 7 $[1+2+3+4+5+6+7=28]$. All perfect numbers, it will be recollected end either in 6 or the 8 of 28. If this feature of the poem, however, is not accidental, it is curious that line-totals in the other sections of the prologue do not seem to have any obvious numerological significance.

Further examples are not difficult to find. One of Heiric's near contemporaries, his pupil, the Benedictine monk Hucbald (c.840–930) composed an 'Eclogue on Baldness' (*Egloga de calvis*)[32] for Charles the Bald. This is in two parts, the eclogue proper being preceded by a dedication to the king. Curtius analyses it thus:[33]

> The dedicatory poem has 54=9 times 6 lines, the eclogue itself 146. 146+54=200. But this is not all! The 146 lines of the eclogue contain an *exordium* and a *conclusio* each of 3 lines. There remain 140 lines = 14 sections of 10 lines. But since the first line of each of the 14 sections is the same and hence represents a sort of burden, performing the function of a sign of division between sections, there remain 9 lines for each section. Thus we find in the eclogue the same number 9 which also predominates in the dedicatory poem. Concerning the 14 finally, be it said that 14=2 times 7. Thus we can see in Hucbald's composition not only round numbers (10, 200), but also combinations of 3, 3 times 3, 2 and 7. No one will wish to deny the deliberate artifice of such a structure.

It may be added that the total number of groups of 9 lines in dedication and eclogue is 20, and the number of lines outside these groups is also 20. The subject is baldness, and every word in the 146 lines of the eclogue begins with *c*, the initial letter not

only of the Latin word *calvus*, 'bald', but also of Charles, the
name of Hucbald's patron (*Carolus calvus*). The initial letters of
Charles' name C C, represent the number 200 which is also the
number of lines in the combined dedication and eclogue.

In these somewhat cryptic lines from the dedication, Hucbald indicates part of his structure, and hints that careful analysis
will easily discover more. Such hints become part of the stock in
trade of the numerological poet:

> *Perspice prudenti perlustrans pectore parva*
> *Munera Musarum miris modulata melodis.*
> *En tibi centenos, ter denos, [bis quos] ternos*
> *Quae 'centum' signat, quae 'calvis' nomine praestat,*
> *Quae frontes pingit confingens cornua lunae,*
> *Quae theatrum format, comprendit littera versus,*
> *Non modo principia his, sed singula verba regirans.*   (*36–42*)

[Examine and survey in your wise heart the little gifts of the
Muses, modulated in marvellous melodies. Behold! the letter
C, which indicates 'one hundred', which begins the word
calvi, which imitates the horns of the moon, adorns beginnings,
and gives a pictorial representation of bald foreheads, which
is shaped like a theatre—this letter is attached to the hundred,
thrice ten, and [twice] three lines of the eclogue, recurring not
only at the beginning of each verse, but in every single word.]

Paraphrases rather than translation is necessary to bring out
the full meaning of the Latin. The section which refers to the
total number of lines is corrupt (giving an apparent sum of 136)
in a way for which I cannot propose any emendation, but even
so, the emphasis on 100, 10, 3 and 2 is obvious, as is also the fact
that the entire passage occupies 7 lines, and that as a whole it is
governed by the nine Muses who control all harmony. 14 9-line
stanzas, to each of which is added the one-line refrain *Carmina,
clarisonae, calvis cantate, Camenae* [Sing, clear-sounding Muses,
songs to the bald], constitute 140 of the 146 lines of the eclogue;
if the refrain is regarded as contributing only once to the line
count, the total becomes 133 rather than 146, in consonance with
the assumed original intention of line 38.

Hucbald, it is interesting to note, was the nephew and pupil of another Carolingian poet, Milo of St Amand (809–871/2), who not only made structural use of numbers in his metrical *Life* of St Amand, but prefixed it with two elaborate Latin acrostics[34]—not alphabetic structures in the sense already dis-cussed, but short poems, 'in which', to quote O E D, 'the initial, the last or the middle letters of the lines, or all of them, taken in order, spell a word, phrase, or sentence, and thus form a *single,* a *double,* or a *triple* acrostic'. Milo's two examples are hexameter poems which form triple acrostics; the second indeed, which may also be read on either diagonal, is a quintuple acrostic. Hexameters are formed by the initial, final, middle, and (in the second poem) diagonal letters, and the effect is completed by the first, last, and middle lines of the poems, which Milo describes as *in specie sanctae crucis editae* [formed in the likeness of the Holy Cross]. The second contains a saltire as well as a regular cross, the whole thus forming a kind of monochromatic Union Jack. The saltire is usually associated with the apostle Andrew, but here probably represents the Greek letter chi (χ), the initial of the word Christ (*Χριστος*). The acrostic, that is to say, represents Christ on the cross, Christ crucified.

Acrostics, at least in these elaborate manifestations written in a single metre, generally have numerological implications. As a consequence of the form, each line necessarily contains the same number of letters, which in turn must also be the total number of lines in the poem as it would usually be read. In Milo's first acrostic, the number of letters and lines is 37, in the second, 35. But there is more to it than this. When initial, middle, final and diagonal hexameters are taken into account, 3 must be added to 37, and 5 to 35, giving in either poem a total of 40 lines. The number 40 has obvious associations with the 40 days of Lent. The cruciform acrostics combine with the numerological reference to form an emblem of austerity, sacrifice and the eucharist, specially appropriate to the *Life* of the saint which follows.

In the second acrostic, the first and last lines are identical with each other, as are the lines formed by initial and final letters, and by the two diagonals. The emblem thus incorporates the repeated text in *Revelation,* where Christ uses the metaphor of the alphabet to declare, 'I am Alpha and Omega, the beginning and the end'. The poem as a whole is an emblem of Christ crucified.

Numerology and the abstractions of musical theory both derive, as has been noted, from *musica mundana,* the harmony of the celestial spheres, which is the Soul of the World.

In such a context it is interesting to note that Hucbald was a theoretical and practical musician of some eminence, author of *De harmonica institutione.*[35] None of his polyphony has survived:

> but he was acknowledged to be an excellent musician. Evidence of this survives in his Gloria trope *Quem vere pia laus,* and in his three *Offices* for St Andrew, St Theoderic, and St Peter. The structure of the last-mentioned anticipates the baroque practice of writing sets of preludes in all possible keys: Hucbald sets the antiphons for matins to each of the eight modes in turn, coming back to the first mode at the ninth and last antiphon.[36]

Hucbald is still sometimes credited with the authorship of another important early theoretical work, *Musica enchiriadis,*[37] which certainly belongs to the same period, and which is chiefly remembered as introducing a clear and workable method of pitch-notation by modifying the Greek letter-notation, inherited from a work mentioned at the end of chapter two, the *De institutione musica* of Boethius. Nearly three hundred signs were thus reduced to a manageable fifteen. The system is now generally known as Daseian notation.

The association in literature of numerological structure with musical form and poet-musicians has a long subsequent history. Denis Stevens, for instance, basing himself on the work of Johannes Alphonsus Huisman,[38] has some interesting things to say about German Minnelieder of the twelfth, thirteenth and fourteenth centuries:[39]

> As poets the Germans were far more cerebral than the French, especially in the matter of balance in planning a long work such

as a *leich*—roughly the German equivalent of the *lai*, which is structurally related to the sequence. A *leich* by the great musician and poet Walther von der Vogelweide (c.1170–c.1230) yields a symmetry in both text and music no less remarkable than that of an isorhythmic motet. In numbers of half-lines (the true unit of measurement) the following figures speak for themselves:

$$12+8 \quad 10+21+10 \quad 12+8 \quad 8+12+8 \quad 10+10 \quad 8+25+8 \quad 8+12$$

$$20 \quad\quad 41 \quad\quad 20 \quad\quad 28 \quad\quad 20 \quad\quad 41 \quad\quad 20$$

$$81 \quad\quad\quad 28 \quad\quad\quad 81$$

$$190$$

Numbers held a mystic power for the mind of medieval man, and this power can be seen at work in countless ways wherever music and poetry join forces. The example from Walther is by no means isolated. Melodically some of these German songs appear delightfully simple, yet this very simplicity often hides a subtle structure only apparent to the listener who is instructed in the art.

Later, in discussing Ars Nova, Gilbert Reaney adds:[40]

If all this preoccupation with form seems more like mathematics than music, the reason is probably that for the medieval man music was a science closely related to arithmetic, and it has to be admitted that the acoustical basis of music is based on numerical relationships. It is not surprising therefore if even practical music was regulated by mathematical principles.

Although Hucbald's *Eclogue* is more a *pièce d'occasion* than any of the other works discussed in this chapter, it demonstrates by virtue of its authorship the link between numerical composition and musical theory and practice. Music provides the closest analogy to numerological form in literature, and is based on very similar principles. During composition and performance, musicians count almost as second nature; medieval musical theory and practice puts almost all its emphasis on music as derivative of mathematics, or mathematics as derivative of music —which has the priority, it is almost impossible to say. Heiric's Platonism is in complete accordance with this point of view. It seems likely that medieval and Renaissance authors tended to write in the same way, and in terms of the same theories, as the musicians their contemporaries. Musical form is abstract; under analysis it may seem excessively formal, yet in the hands of a great master it is capable of the most profound intellectual and emotional effects. Numerological form in literature is sometimes dismissed as at best a decorative excrescence, alternatively as something necessarily hampering creative expression, at worst as mere coincidence, warped ingenuity on the part of the reader— even, an intrinsically impossible illusion. The analogy of music[41] may help to show the inadequacy of these views.

4

The Transition to the Vernaculars

Queste del Saint Graal—Vita Nuova

The period from the sixth to the ninth century saw the establishment of numerological composition in Latin verse and prose.
Nowadays it is almost a commonplace to say that the medieval
vernacular literatures derive most of their essential features from
earlier medieval Latin literature. This is certainly the case with
numerological composition. The earliest vernacular instance
known to me, the French *Vie de Saint Alexis*,[1] is considerably
later than any of the Latin examples already quoted (it was composed about 1040), while at the same time it resembles them in
several different ways. It is, for example, a saint's *Life* as are the
poems of Heiric, Milo, and also, in a rather different style, the
Navigatio Sancti Brendani Abbatis. The emphasis therefore is on
the subjugation of the flesh, exemplified by Alexis' desertion of
his wife on their wedding night in Rome, to begin a life of
seclusion and poverty, first at the Syrian port of Laodicea
(*Lalice*), then at Edessa (*Alsis*) in Mesopotamia. After seventeen
years his sanctity is proclaimed by a statue of the Virgin in
Edessa. To avoid popular applause, he returns unrecognised to
his father's house in Rome, where he is permitted to continue his
austerities under the stairs until his death seventeen years later.
'Feeling the approach of death, he inscribes on a piece of parch-
ment the story of his life, and his identity is recognised after his
death.'[2]

The structure of the poem is based on the number 5
(Heiric's Pentad); it is composed in 125 (5^3) 5-line deca-
syllabic stanzas, each line containing 5 feet. The total number of

feet is therefore 5^5. The structure thus embodies the traditional significance of the pentacle or pentangle, a significance long afterwards expounded by the anonymous author of the fourteenth-century English poem, *Sir Gawain and the Green Knight*:[3]

It is a symbol which Solomon conceived once
To betoken true faith, which it is entitled to,
For it is a figure which has five points,
And each line overlaps and is bound with another;
And it is endless everywhere, and the English call it,
As I have heard, the Endless Knot.
Therefore it goes with Sir Gawain and his gleaming armour,
For, ever faithful in five things, each in fivefold manner,
Gawain was known as a good man and, like gold well-refined,
He was devoid of all villainy, every virtue displaying
     In the field.
   Thus this Pentangle new
   He carried on coat and shield,
   As a man of troth most true
   And knightly name annealed.

First he was found faultless in his five wits.
Next, his five fingers never failed the knight,
And all his trust on earth was in the five wounds
Which came to Christ on the Cross, as the Creed tells.
And whenever the bold man was busy on the battlefield,
Through all other things he thought on this,
That his prowess all depended on the five pure Joys
That the holy Queen of Heaven had of her Child.
Accordingly the courteous knight had that queen's image
Etched on the inside of his armoured shield,
So that when he beheld her, his heart did not fail.
The fifth five I find the famous man practised
Were—Liberality and Lovingkindness leading the rest;
Then his Continence and Courtesy, which were never
     corrupted;
And Piety, the surpassing virtue. These pure five

Were more firmly fixed on that fine man
Than on any other, and every multiple,
Each interlocking with another, had no end,
Being fixed to five points which never failed,
Never assembling on one side, nor sundering either,
With no end at any angle; nor can I find
Where the design started or proceeded to its end.
Thus on his shining shield the shape of this knot
Was royally rendered in red gold on gules.
That is the pure Pentangle, so called by people wise
    In lore.   [Part Two, stanzas 6 and 7]

Five is thus particularly appropriate for any poem or prose work concerned with the subjugation of the flesh. This significance, it should be noted, is distinct from, but does not contradict any other already discussed. It is based on the idea that in the five-fold universe (Father, Son, Spirit, Angels, Lower Creation) the appropriate place for the five senses is the base of the hierarchy.

The Marian references in the passage from *Sir Gawain and the Green Knight* are particularly relevant for a *Life* of St Alexis, whose sanctity was initially revealed by a statue of the Virgin.

As vital as the pentad is the fact that Alexis devoted a total of 34 years to his austerities. Christ was in his 34th year at the time of the Crucifixion; the period denotes the identification with Christ at which the saint aimed. The image of the Virgin speaks in the 34th stanza of the poem at a time when Alexis had devoted 17 years to his austerities:

Quant tut sun quor en ad si afermet,
Que ja, sum voil, n'istrat de la citied,
Deus fist l'imagine pur sue amur parler
Al servitor ki serveit al alter.
Ço li cumandet: 'Apele l'hume Deu!   [170–5]

[When he is convinced with all his heart that henceforth by choice he will no longer leave the city, God, because of his love of him, had the statue speak to the attendant who served at the altar. It commanded him: 'Call the man of God!']

Earlier, the 17th stanza of the poem had described the arrival of the saint at Laodicea to begin his austerities; the first period of 17 years is thus covered in 17 stanzas. The second period occupies 34 stanzas, completed when a good servant tells Euphemian, the father of Alexis, that the man of God, for whom Pope Innocent and the Emperors Arcadius and Honorius are desperately searching, has just died in his house:

> *Li boens serganz ki·l serveit volentiers,*
> *Il le nunçat sum pedre Eufemien;*
> *Suef l'apelet, si li ad conseilet.*
> *'Sire,' dist il, 'Morz est tes provenders,*
> *E ço sai dire qu'il fut bons cristiens.'*   [*336–40*]

[The worthy servant who served him willingly, he announced it to his father, Euphemian. He calls him softly and suggests what he might do. 'My lord,' he said, 'The man you were providing for is dead, and I can tell you that he was a good Christian.']

The people of Rome recognised the saint's merits and crowded round his body to pray for his intercession on their behalf.

The narrative of events from the beginning of the saint's austerities to his recognition by the Roman populace thus occupies 85 stanzas [17 + 34 + 34], leaving 40 for the introduction and conclusion. As has already been demonstrated, 40 is itself a number closely connected with austerity, suffering, and especially with preparation and anticipation. The number it will be recollected, was especially important in *Navigatio Sancti Brendani Abbatis,* as earlier in both the Old and New Testaments.

5 reappears in the later mystical French prose romance, the *Queste del Saint Graal,*[4] the 'Quest of the Holy Grail', composed, perhaps in a Cistercian monastery, somewhere between the years 1215 and 1230 as part of the enormous meticulously constructed work generally known as the Prose *Lancelot.*[5] This is constructed not in 5 but 15 chapters of unequal length, which narrate the attempts of various knights of Arthur's Round Table to complete the quest of the Holy Grail, the vessel from which Christ served his disciples at the institution of the Eucharist, the

Last Supper, and in which the final drops of blood from his crucified body were caught and preserved by Joseph of Arima‚ thea. Three knights—Bors [*Boorz*], Perceval and Galahad [*Galaad*]—successfully reach Corbenic, the castle in Britain where the Grail has found a temporary home, and afterwards accompany it in Solomon's Ship to the spiritual palace at Sarras, whence finally it is removed to heaven. Galahad and Perceval die at Sarras, but Bors returns to Arthur's court.

Among the other knights, Lancelot partly completes the quest, but the remainder, notably Gawain [*Gauvain*], fail miserably.

As Gawain's dream in chapter 8 indicates, 150 knights made up the complement of the Round Table, of whom two approached and one fully achieved the grade of perfection necessary for the successful completion of the quest of the Holy Grail. The 15 chapters correspond at one and the same time to the 150 and to the 3. $150 = 15 \times 10$; $3 \times 5 = 15$, and $5 =$ spiritual perfection as exemplified by Bors, Perceval and Galahad. 3, as will be indicated below, is itself of structural importance. 15 again is the sum of the first 5 integers ($1+2+3+4+5=15$), and is thus a glorified form of 5, just as 10, the Tetractys ($1+2+3+4 = 10$) was in Pythagorean belief a glorified form of 4. 15 is thus equivalent to 5, which represents perfection primarily because it represents the 5 talents of the parable [*Matthew 25, 14–30*], which is retold—significantly in chapter 5—to Lancelot, who once possessed all 5, but hid them in the ground:

> I know that I shall be judged like the wicked servant who hid his talent in the ground. All my life long I have served His enemy and have waged war on Him with the arms of sin. And I have gone to my death down that wide road which at the outset seems so smooth and honeyed and is the portal and path of sin.

The hermit in chapter 5 interprets the talents once possessed by Lancelot as (1) Beauty (2) Understanding (3) Courage (4) Skill in battle (5) Good fortune, all vital attributes of the secular knight. One by one they have deserted him until he is left

in his present miserable state. But a more theological interpretation is present in chapter 7, where the 5 virtues of (1) Virginity
(2) Humility (3) Long suffering (4) Rectitude and (5) Charity
are said to have belonged to Lancelot, but to have been replaced
primarily by Lust and Pride, which first expelled Virginity and
Humility, then combined to drive out the others, although there
is still some possibility of restoration.

In the course of the narrative of the five days spent by Lancelot
at the hermitage, the hermit who tells the parable of the talents
uses direct speech on 15 occasions, 14 in chapter 5 and 1 in
chapter 7. This device is thrice used elsewhere, once with each of
the perfect knights, and usually indicates direct divine communication which is only partially or with difficulty recognised
as such, most obviously in the case of the priest who uses a supernatural ship (which later will convey the 3 Grail knights) to
visit Perceval on his deserted island. 15 of this priest's utterances
are reported in direct speech, to the last of which Perceval replies
in a moment of illumination:[6]

> I must believe you are no mortal man but a spiritual being. I
> know beyond question that if you stayed with me for ever I
> should know neither hunger nor thirst. Indeed, if I dared speak
> the words, I would say you are the Living Bread that comes
> down from heaven, which is a pledge of everlasting life to all
> who partake worthily thereof.

> [*et se je l'osoie dire, je diroie que vos estes li Pains vis qui descent des
> ciex , dont nus ne menjue dignement qui perdurablement ne vive.*]

At this the 'good man' vanishes, leaving his vessel to convey
Perceval to the meeting with Bors and Galahad. Perceval
clearly has been granted a moment of spiritual insight, the
immediate occasion for which is the 15 utterances of his visitor,
who is Christ, or at the very least one of his angels.

Chapter 6 is entirely devoted to Perceval's 'adventures' (the
word—O.F. *aventure*—is used in the sense 'actual events or trains
of events the primary significance of which is spiritual'. It bears
only a superficial relationship to the modern meaning). Equally,
chapter 9 is devoted to the very different character and adventures

of Bors. The hermit whom he meets is a more prosaic figure than the priest in the boat, rather as Bors himself is a more prosaic character than Perceval. Divine grace, we may say, takes a form appropriate to the recipient, here that of 'a very aged man wearing a monk's habit and riding along on an ass, quite alone, without squire or servant'. For a reader sensitive to the stylistic subtleties of the *Queste*, the brief description at once raises the possibility that the aged man is more than he appears to be, and his first words contain what should, I suggest, be taken as a reference to Lancelot, Bors' cousin, whose moral illness and encounter with this same hermit has already been described in chapters 5 and 7:

> Bors asked him then where he came from thus alone.
> 'I have been to visit a servant of mine who is ill, and who used to do my errands.'

The combination of humility and authority in the words and figure of the hermit is continued throughout his 15 remarks, which include the command to Bors to eat only bread and water until he is seated at the table of the Holy Grail, his affirmation that Bors *will* sit there, and his gift of a white frock (*une cote blanche*, the Cistercian habit) for Bors to wear in place of a shirt. The final emphasis is on the Eucharist, towards which Bors maintains a steady faith, quite different from Perceval's sudden leap of insight, but which nevertheless brings on a fit of weeping. Bors' mind and heart are both profoundly engaged:

> 'Bors, do you see what I am holding?'
> 'Yes, indeed, Sir. I see that you are holding my Saviour and Redeemer under the guise of bread. I should not be looking on Him in this wise were it not that my eyes, being mortal clay, and thus unapt to discern the things of the spirit, do not permit my seeing Him any other way, but rather cloak His true appearance. For I have no doubt that what I look on now is truly flesh and truly man and wholly God.'
> At these words he was overmastered by weeping.

Bors does not detect his Saviour in the figure of the hermit, but it is certain that the author intended his readers to have a keener insight, stimulated by his use of the number 15.

Galahad too has a 15-fold revelation, the beginning of which is delayed until his arrival at Corbenic in chapter *15*, and which later in the same chapter is completed at Sarras. Throughout, Bors and Perceval are present, to indicate, it may be, that the nature and accomplishment of both is consummated in the perfection of Galahad. The 15 utterances are not delivered by a hermit; six are ascribed to a 'voice', the source of which is heavenly; five come from the son of Joseph of Arimathea, Josephus, the first Christian bishop, consecrated by Our Lord himself, and dead for more than 300 years, who continues his office in heaven. As Josephus is elevating the Host during the celebration of Mass at Corbenic, 'there descended from above a figure like to a child, whose countenance glowed and blazed as bright as fire; and he entered into the bread, which quite distinctly took on human form before the eyes of those assembled there.' (With this, contrast Bors' expression of his own imperfect vision, quoted above). Josephus, after replacing the Host in the Grail and making one more utterance, vanishes. 'Then the companions, raising their eyes, saw the figure of a man appear from out of the Holy Vessel, unclothed, and bleeding from his hands and feet and side'—Christ in the Eucharist, who serves them from the Grail, and delivers to Galahad the 4 utterances which make up the total of 15.

15 is at once 3×5 and, as the sum of the first 5 integers $(1+2+3+4+5=15)$, a glorified form of 5. One significance (in the *Queste*, that is to say) of 5 in isolation appears to be the individual perfection of the Person in the Trinity. The primary significance of 15 may thus be the perfection of the Trinity, God in three Persons, as symbolised in the Eucharist, a perfection which partially emerges in the incident of the men which forms part of Lancelot's adventure [chapter *14*] at Corbenic:

> So he let his gaze run round the room and observed the Holy Vessel standing beneath a cloth of bright red samite upon a silver table. And all around were ministering angels, some swinging silver censers, others holding lighted candles, crosses

and other altar furnishings, each and every one intent upon some service. Before the Holy Vessel was an aged man in priestly vestments, engaged to all appearance in the consecration of the mass. When he came to elevate the host, Lancelot thought he saw, above his outstretched hands [*il fu avis a Lancelot que desus les mains au preudome en haut avoit*], three men, two of whom were placing the youngest in the hands of the priest who raised him aloft as though he were showing him to the people.

Lancelot's vision is imperfect, but corresponds at once to the participation of the three Persons of the Trinity in the Eucharist, and to the relationship between the youngest Grail knight, Galahad, and the two elder, Bors and Perceval. God the Son transubstantiates the eucharistic elements. Galahad is a type of God the Son; a more distant correspondence is that between Bors, the cousin of Galahad's father, Lancelot, and God the Father, and between Perceval and God the Holy Spirit. The 3 earthly knights in some sense correspond to the three Persons of the Trinity: the triple perfection of the number 13 also applies to them.

Lancelot fails to understand what he has imperfectly seen, and as a consequence he is punished by the fit in which he lies unconscious for 24 days, representing the 24 years during which he has lived in sin. Here as elsewhere the number 24 represents time and temporal things as opposed to eternity. (The Greek alphabet from alpha to omega, it will be recollected contains 24 letters, and there are, of course, 24 hours in the day.) The period of severance from the body becomes for Lancelot, however, an instant in eternity, from which he is reluctant to return:

It was around noon on the twenty-fourth day that he opened his eyes. At the sight of the people gathered round he set up a great lamentation, crying: 'Ah! God, why didst thou waken me so soon? I was far happier now than ever I shall be again! Ah! gracious Lord Jesus Christ, where dwells the man so blessed by fortune and above reproach that he could contemplate Thy glorious mysteries and set his gaze there where my sinful sight was darkened and my eyes blinded, that had been sullied by looking on the midden of this world [*la tres grant ordure dou monde*]?'

5 and 3 often occur elsewhere in the course of the narrative. There are, for instance, the 5 inscriptions which adorn the Ship of Solomon and its contents;[7] 3 of these are on the sword of David. There are the 3 great fellowships listed in chapter 6, the Table of Jesus Christ and his Apostles, the Table of the Holy Grail at which Josephus presided, and the Round Table with the Siege Perilous, eventually occupied by Galahad. There are 3 swords, the Sword of David or Sword of the Strange Belt, presented to Galahad by Perceval's sister [chapter *12*]: the Sword in the Stone, worn first by Galahad, afterwards by Perceval [chapter *12*]: and the Sword that was Broken, restored by Galahad and worn by Bors [chapter *5*]. If the entire narrative is divided into 5 sections each of 3 chapters, the first concludes [chapter *3*] with Galahad, the second [chapter *6*] with Perceval, the third [chapter *9*] with Bors; the fourth [chapter *12*] is built round the sacrificial virgin figure of Perceval's sister, a feminine equivalent of the Grail knights. The fifth finally [chapter *15*] centres on Galahad, but with the other Grail knights present, and the body of Perceval's sister arriving for burial at Sarras.

Each of the first 9 chapters, forming the first three sections of the *Queste,* contains some numerical indication of its position and significance. Chapter *1* is built round the appearance of the unique figure of Galahad, to occupy the Siege Perilous and win the Sword in the Stone, reserved for the best knight in the world. Chapter *2* ends where the road forks in 2 directions at a cross with the inscription:

'Give heed, thou knight that goest about seeking adventure: behold two roads, one to thy left, the other to thy right. The left-hand road thou shalt not take, for he that enters therein must be second to none if he would follow it to the end: and if thou take the right-hand road, haply thou mayest soon perish.'

Chapter *3* begins with the emphasis still on 2; the 2-day

journey of Melias leading to his overthrow; the successful battle of Galahad with 2 knights; the 2 sins of Melias which caused his overthrow. Galahad however stays 3 days with the wounded Melias at the abbey to which he takes him; he receives a 3-fold warning as he approaches the Castle of Maidens; he unhorses 3 of the 7 knights who attack him. Chapter 3 contains 3 episodes; the misadventure of Melias, avenged in episode 2 by Galahad, followed by the episode of the Castle of Maidens.

In the brief chapter 4 it is revealed that 4 years have passed since Gawain last went to confession. 4, it will be remembered, is a number often associated by way of the 4 elements, the 4 seasons, the 4 cardinal points, with the temporal world and its chief inhabitant, the human body, both subjects which occupy the forefront of Gawain's attention.

Chapter 5 is distinguished by the application of the parable of the five talents to Lancelot. The five talents are a specific example of the perfection implicit in the number, but the application indicates that even in apparent human perfection lurks the possibility of eternal failure.

The action of chapter 6 occupies 6 days. 6 is a multiple of 3 ($2 \times 3 = 6$) and perfect in a strictly mathematical sense (see chapter 3 above); the book appropriately concerns itself with Perceval, the 2nd of the 3 Grail knights.

Chapter 7 includes Lancelot's dream of 7 kings—Narpus, Nascien, Elian, Isaiah, Jonaan, Lancelot 1 and Ban—who are his own immediate ancestors, each of whom won the redemption which at this point it seems unlikely their descendant will attain. It may be significant that by the twelfth and thirteenth centuries 7 had become preeminently the number of humanity,[8] composed, as it is, of 4, the number of the body and 3, the number of the soul, and expresses the union of man's double nature. Just as Galahad is a type of Christ, so Lancelot is of Adam, fallen man.

Chapter 8 begins with the meeting of Gawain and Hector— ironically, since they later fail to repent, on the day of the penitent sinner, St Mary Magdalene (July 22nd). The subsequent action occupies 8 days with the significant events taking place on the night preceding the 8th day, and in the course of the day itself.

(In the *Queste* generally a night is regarded as part of the following rather than the preceding day). Again, irony is probably intended. The number 8 was 'the number of the new life. It comes after seven which marks the limit assigned to the life of man and to the duration of the world. The number eight is like an octave in music with which all begins once more. It is the symbol of the new life, of the final resurrection and of that anticipated resurrection implied in baptism.'

Émile Mâle, whom I quote,[9] is discussing the octagonal form of the baptismal font in a Gothic cathedral, but his words here as elsewhere have an obvious relevance to the *Queste,* a literary work contemporary with the cathedrals. The hermit offers Gawain the opportunity, even at so late a stage, of a new life:

> Gawain, it is a long time since you were knighted, and in all these years you have done little enough for your Maker. You are an old tree, bare now of leaves and fruit. Bear this in mind, if nothing else, that Our Lord should have the pith and bark, since the enemy has had the flower and the fruit.

Gawain sees himself as postponing rather than rejecting the offer. The true state of affairs is revealed by the triviality of his reason for so doing:

> 'Sir,' replied Sir Gawain, 'had I the leisure to talk to you I would do so gladly. But you see my companion making off down the hill, and I must needs go too. But believe me, I shall return as soon as opportunity allows, for I am most anxious to speak with you in private.'

The hermit, it may be added, addresses 8 remarks in direct speech to Gawain and Hector. The parallel and contrast with the 15 remarks made by a hermit to each of the Grail knights and to Lancelot is enough to suggest that here too we have direct divine communication, to which Gawain, unlike the others, fails to give even the most limited recognition.

$8 = 2 \times 4$, and Gawain's earlier experiences, it will be remembered, were narrated in chapter 4. The number symbolism of the *Queste* is mainly biblical, but here it should perhaps also be remembered that 'the Pythagoreans, indeed, called the number eight Justice'.[10]

9 is another multiple of 3 ($3 \times 3 = 9$), and chapter 9 is appropriately devoted to the adventures of the 3rd Grail knight, Bors. They are 9 in number: (i) the meeting, already discussed, between Bors and the hermit; (ii) the symbolic episode of the great bird reviving its young at the cost of its own life; (iii) the episode of the two sisters and King Love's inheritance; (iv) the vision of the two birds, prefiguring the encounter with the monk on the black horse and the suicidal lady; (v) the vision of the rotten tree, prefiguring the aborted combat of Bors and his brother Lionel; (vi) the vision of the two lilies, prefiguring the rescue by Bors of the kidnapped girl; (vii) the death of the hermit; (viii) the death of Calogrenant; (ix) the divine voice halting the combat with Lionel and directing Bors to Perceval's ship.

9, in effect, is the last individual number in the decad: 10 marks the return to unity with the arrival of the 3 Grail knights and Perceval's sister at Solomon's Ship. 9 is at once the limit and (closely linked as it is to 3 and unity) the consummation of number. Its intrinsic arithmetical qualities combine with such associations as the 9 celestial spheres and the 9 hierarchies of angels to make 9 prominent, not only in the *Queste,* but generally in medieval numerology.

This may best perhaps be illustrated by the *Vita Nuova*[11] of Dante (1265–1321). In chapters XXIX and XXX he explains how the number was closely allied to the central figure of Beatrice:

> Nevertheless, as the number nine, which number hath often had mention in what hath gone before (and not, as it might appear, without reason), seems also to have borne a part in the manner of her death: it is therefore right that I should say somewhat thereof. And for this cause, having first said what was the part it bore herein, I will afterwards point out a reason

which made that this number was so closely allied unto my lady.

xxx. I say, then, that according to the division of time in Arabia, her most noble spirit departed from among us in the first hour of the ninth day of the month; and according to the division of time in Syria, in the ninth month of the year: seeing that Tisrin 1, which with us is October, is there the first month. Also she was taken from among us in that year of our reckoning (to wit, of the years of our Lord) in which the perfect number [10—the return to unity] was nine times multiplied within that century wherein she was born into the world: which is to say, the thirteenth century of Christians.

And touching the reason why this number was so closely allied unto her, it may peradventure be this. According to Ptolemy (and also to the Christian verity), the revolving heavens are nine; and according to the common opinion among astrologers, these nine heavens together have influence over the earth. Wherefore it would appear that this number was thus allied unto her for the purpose of signifying that, at her birth, all these nine heavens were at perfect unity with each other as to their influence. This is one reason that may be brought, but more narrowly considering, and according to the infallible truth, this number was her own self: that is to say, by similitude. As thus. The number three is the root of the number nine; seeing that without the interposition of any other number, being multiplied merely by itself, it produceth nine as we manifestly perceive that three times three are nine. Thus, three being of itself the factor of nine, and the Factor of Miracles being of Himself Three Persons (to wit: the Father, the Son, and the Holy Spirit), which, being Three, are also One: this lady was accompanied by the number nine to the end that men might clearly perceive her to be a nine, that is, a miracle, whose only root is the Holy Trinity. It may be that a more subtle person would find for this thing a reason of greater subtilty: but such is the reason that I find, and that liketh me best.

Dante indicates that death was not the sole occasion on

which 9 seemed to govern his relation with Beatrice. He was 9 years old when he first saw her. 'She appeared to me at the beginning of her ninth year almost, and I saw her almost at the end of my ninth year' [chapter 11]. 9 years later, in the 9th hour of the day, she first bestowed on him her miracle-working salutation, and his subsequent vision of 'a lord of terrible aspect' [*uno signore, di pauroso aspetto*], the God of Love himself, took place in 'the fourth hour (which is to say, the first of the nine last hours) of the night' [chapter 111]. Chapter VI tells how he composed a *serventese* containing the names of sixty beautiful ladies, and 'found my lady's name would not stand otherwise than *ninth* in order among the names of these ladies'. In chapter XII the vision of the youth in very white raiment, which follows the denial of Beatrice's salutation, occurs during the 9th hour of the day. Chapter XXIII tells of the 'imaginations' which overcame him on the 9th day of an illness. The climax is a vision of angels carrying the soul of Beatrice to Heaven:

Levava gli occhi miei bagnati in pianti,
  E vedea (che parean pioggia di manna)
  Gli angeli che tornavan suso in cielo,
  Ed una nuvoletta avean davanti,
  Dopo la qual gridavan tutti: 'Osanna'.   [59–61]

[Then lifting up mine eyes, as the tears came,
I saw the angels, like a rain of manna,
  In a long flight flying back Heavenward;
Having a little cloud in front of them,
  After the which they went and said 'Hosanna'.]

Several things are to be noted about *Donna pietosa e di novella etate,* from which this last example is taken. The poem is one of 3 completed *canzoni,* the longest and most sustained individual compositions in the *Vita Nuova.* (The others are *Donne, ch'avete intelletto d'amore* in chapter XIX and *Gli occhi dolenti per pietà del core* in chapter XXXII.) It has been demonstrated[12] that the 3 have themselves an important function, discussed below, in the numerological structure. For the moment, however, it suffices

to note that *Donna pietosa e di novella etate* immediately precedes
chapter XXIV, Dante's encounter with the lady Giovanna
(Joan), who was called Primavera (Spring), and that Giovanna
in turn was immediately followed by Beatrice. In the two ladies
Dante sees types of John (Giovanni) the Baptist, who came
before [*prima verra,* 'she will come first'] Christ, with whom
Beatrice is implicitly paralleled. The 'vain imaginations', so-
called, of the preceding *canzone,* in which the death of Beatrice is
associated with the Ascension, the last event of Christ's earthly
sojourn, are completed in the prose of chapter XXIV with the
reference to the voice crying in the wilderness which heralded the
beginning of Christ's mission. In the sonnet which completes
chapter XXIV the point is somewhat disguised, out of regard,
Dante says, for his chief friend, the poet Guido Cavalcanti
(c.1255–1300), whose heart, he believed, 'still regarded the
beauty of her that was called Spring'. Chapter XXIII nevertheless remains as the prologue (or perhaps rather the inverted
epilogue) of chapter XXIV. 23, in other words, is not so much a
free integer as 24–1.

This being granted, a certain regular sequence will be found
in Dante's references to 9, a sequence which calls attention to
another number from the decad. The total number of references,
or closely associated clusters of references, to the number is 6. The
earliest occur in chapters II and III. $2 \times 3 = 6$, and the third
occurs in chapter VI, where also is mentioned the *serventese* containing the names of 60 (6×10) ladies. The fourth is in chapter
XII, and $12 = 2 \times 6$. The fifth is in chapter XXIII, but, as has
been seen, $23 = 24–1$, and $24 = 4 \times 6$. Chapter XXIX, which
introduces the number for the 6th time, is correspondingly to be
regarded as a prologue to the analysis, already quoted, which
forms chapter XXX, and $30 = 5 \times 6$.

The recurrence of 9 thus serves indirectly to emphasise 6,
a number whose properties have already been discussed, and
which are strikingly applicable to Beatrice (a further possible
reference is mentioned below). In addition, the death of Beatrice
is announced in line 56 of the *canzone*:

Ed uom m'apparve scolorito e fioco,
Dicendomi: Che fai? non sai novella?
Morta è la donna tua, ch'era sì bella. [54–6]

[And I was ware of one, hoarse and tired-out,
Who ask'd of me: 'Hast thou not heard it said?
Thy lady, she that was so fair, is dead.']

$56 = 7 \times 8$, and in the *Somnium Scipionis,* which Dante knew well, it is declared[13] to be a number of great destinal significance. The younger is told by the elder Scipio that the product of 7 and 8 will round out his destiny when his age had 'completed seven times eight recurring circuits of the sun'—when he is 56 years old, that is to say, the age in fact at which he died. Correspondingly, the death of Beatrice is unequivocally mentioned for the first time in line 56 of the *canzone,* and it is probably significant that the theme recurs with the number and a change of emotional emphasis echoing the overall movement of the *Vita Nuova,* in the equiva-lent line of the third of the completed *canzoni, Gli occhi dolenti per pietà del core*:

Poscia piangendo, sol nel mio lamento
Chiamo Beatrice; e dico: Or, se' tu morta!
E mente ch'io la chiamo, mi conforta. [54–6]

[Afterward, calling with a sore lament
On Beatrice, I ask, 'Canst thou be dead?'
And calling on her, I am comforted.]

Not only 6, then, but 7 and 8 also are assigned some function in the structure.

It has long been recognised that the 3 completed *canzoni* play a part in the structure of the *Vita Nuova.* They appear, with no immediately perceptible regularity, in chapters xix, xxiii and xxxii. The entire book, however, contains 31 poems, of which *Donne, ch'avete intelletto d'amore* is 11th, *Donna pietosa e di novella etate* is 16th, and *Gli occhi dolenti per pietà del core* is 21st. The regularity of the sequence immediately becomes more obvious: it is

10 poems: *Canzone*: 4 poems: *Canzone*: 4 poems: *Canzone*:
10 poems.

To a degree this already emphasises 9 in the middle sequence,
but C. S. Singleton[14] increased the emphasis by setting the first
and last poems apart as proem and epilogue, thus giving

Proem: 9 poems: *Canzone*: 4 poems: *Canzone*: 4 poems:
Canzone: 9 poems: Epilogue,

even ultimately

1 : 9 : 1 : 9 : 1 : 9 : 1

This may now, I think, be taken as established, but at the
same time puzzling, because it so entirely ignores the system of
numbering by chapters, which appears to have originated with
Dante, and which presumably he intended to carry some
significance. The book contains 43 chapters of varied length, and
one may, without undue subjectivity, single out 9 of these as
particularly striking, and so likely to be structural. Chapter III
narrates the first occasion on which Beatrice gave Dante her
miraculous salutation, and his subsequent vision of the God of
Love. In chapter IX Dante meets Amor by the light of day:
'Wherefore it came to pass that he who ruled me by virtue of my
most gentle lady was made visible to my mind, in the light habit
of a traveller, coarsely fashioned. He appeared to me troubled,
and looked always on the ground, saving only that sometimes
his eyes were turned towards a river which was clear and rapid,
and which flowed along the path I was taking.' (The river,
which probably represents the passage of time, recurs in chapter
XIX.) The episode is completed when in chapter X Beatrice
withdraws her salutation. Chapter XII describes Dante's grief
at the loss, and includes the dream in which Amor defines himself in terms which parody the ancient definition of deity:[15] *Ego
tanquam centrum circuli, cui simili modo se habent circumferentiae partes:
tu autem non sic.* [I am as the centre of a circle, to the which all
parts of the circumference bear an equal relation, but with thee it
is not thus.] Chapters XIX and XXIII contain the first and
second of the three *canzoni,* the first followed in chapter XX by a
sonnet defining Love in reminiscence of the earlier poet, Guido
Guinicelli (c.1235–1276), whom Dante regarded as his master,

at least in lyric poetry. Chapter XXIX not only tells the death of Beatrice, but begins the discussion of 9, completed in chapter XXX. Chapter XXXII contains the third *canzone*. Chapter XXXIX describes the incipient faithlessness of Dante, from which in chapter XL he is redeemed by a noontide 'visible phantasy, wherein I seemed to behold the most gracious Beatrice, habited in that crimson raiment which she had worn when I first beheld her; also she seemed to me of the same tender age as then'. Chapter XLIII, finally, mentions 'a very wonderful vision' which may be the first hint of the *Divina Commedia*.

It will be noticed, first, that there is a total of 9 significant points, and that the final digit of 7 of the 9 chapters indicated (3, 9, 19, 23, 29, 39, 43) is either 9 or its square root 3. The remaining numbers, 2 and 32, each end in 2. The 9-fold sequence thus forms a regular pattern of final digits:

3 9 2 9 3 9 2 9 3

Nor is this all. The first chapters singled out are III and IX. 3 + 9 = 12, and the next chapter of special significance is XII. The action of chapter IX is completed, as is the decad, in chapters X, and 10 + 9 = 19. Chapter XIX is next on the list, and is completed, with the second decad, in chapter XX. 20 + 3 = 23: 20 + 9 = 29: 20 + 3 + 9 = 32; chapters XXIII, XXIX and XXXII are next to be singled out. The action of chapter XXIX is completed in chapter XXX, which marks the third decad, 30 + 9 = 39, and chapter XXXIX, next on the list, is completed by chapter XL, the fourth decad. 40 + 3 = 43 and chapter XLIII completes the work. It is notable how the successive decads are emphasised almost as much as the 9s and 3s.

The chapter numbers also function in a slightly different, less subjective, way. The first 28 chapters are concerned with the earthly life of Beatrice, the remaining 15 with events after her death. Dante himself separates the two parts by leaving the *canzone* begun in chapter XXVIII a mere fragment: by the isolated biblical quotation, *Quomodo sedet sola civitas plena populo! facta est quasi vidua domina gentium,* which begins chapter XXIX, and by his repositioning of the formal analyses (the 'divisions') before rather than after the poems which they accompany. He notes the change in the division of the first poem in the final sequence, *Gli occhi dolenti per pietà del core* in chapter XXXII: 'That this poem may seem to remain the more widowed at its close, I will divide it before writing it, and this method I will observe henceforward.'

It has already been noted that 28 and 15 are both numbers of some power and significance. 28 is the second perfect number, generated by the summation of its factors ($1+2+4+7+14=28$). Alastair Fowler's comment,[16] though made of another poem, is appropriate. 'Because it neither exceeded its divisions nor fell short, a perfect number symbolised virtue: symbolically a desirable total for the years of a life. . . . In Biblical exegesis 28 denoted the dimensions of the Temple, so that the completion of the spirit's dwelling would be meant.' All three meanings are present in the *Vita Nuova*.

The earlier parts of this chapter have demonstrated the association of 15 with the ascended Christ and the Trinity. It may be added that the associations, also previously discussed, of 40 may help to explain why the posthumous vision of Beatrice, in some sense the climax of the work, appears in chapter XL.

Several individual numbers thus play a part in the structure of the *Vita Nuova*, but 9 remains the most important, because most often emphasised and most often directly associated with Beatrice. Dante is also aware of the association, derived from the *Celestial Hierarchy*[17] of Dionysius the pseudo-Areopagite, of 9 with the angelic orders. He seems to have known the derivation of the word 'angel' from Greek ἄγγελος, 'a (divine) messenger'. To some degree it is in this sense that Beatrice in the *Vita Nuova* is regarded as an angel, though the concept is not immediately revealed in its fullness, and differs greatly, it must be remembered, from that of Coventry Patmore, for instance, in *The Angel in the House*.[18] Dante's angels are more formidable than their Victorian counterparts. Beatrice's angelic status is implied almost from the beginning in the importance accorded to her salutation, almost like that of Gabriel to Mary in *Luke 1.28-9*.

In chapter II, the statement that Beatrice is 'the youngest of the angels' (*quest' angiola giovannissima*) is supported by the devastating effect of her presence on Dante's faculties, an effect often mentioned in subsequent chapters:

At that moment, I say most truly that the spirit of life, which hath its dwelling in the secretest chamber of the heart, began to tremble so violently that the least pulses of my body shook therewith; and in trembling it said these words: *Ecce deus fortior me, qui veniens dominabitur mihi.* At that moment the animate spirit, which dwelleth in the lofty chambers whither all the senses carry their perceptions, was filled with wonder, and speaking more especially unto the spirits of the eyes, said these words: *Apparuit jam beatitudo vestra.* At that moment the natural spirit, which dwelleth there where our nourishment is administered, began to weep, and in weeping said these words: *Heu miser! quia frequenter impeditus ero deinceps.*

The effect of Beatrice's presence on Dante's triple soul—the spirited, the rational and the appetitive—is like that of Gabriel on Zacharias [*Luke 1.11–12*]: 'And there appeared unto him an angel of the Lord standing on the right side of the altar of incense. And when Zacharias saw him, he was troubled and fear fell upon him.' As a consequence of this visitation, it will be remembered, Zacharias was stricken with dumbness, a state in which he remained for more than nine months until at circumcision the occasion came for naming his newly-born son, John, eventually the Baptist. Dante's affliction is akin to that of Zacharias.

The first of the three great *canzone, Donne, ch'avete intelletto d'amore* (chapter XIX) [Ladies that have intelligence of love], begins to elaborate the concept. The word *intelletto,* 'understanding, intellect, reason', hints at a connection between some ladies at least and the angelic intelligences, a link which is developed in terms of Beatrice in the second and third stanzas:

Angelo chiama in divino intelletto,
  E dice: Sire, nel mondo si vede
  Meraviglia nell'atto, che procede
  Da un'anima, che fin quassù risplende.

Lo cielo, che non have altro difetto
Che d'aver lei, al suo Signor la chiede
E ciascun santo ne grida mercede.
Sola pietà nostra parte difende;
Chè parla Iddio, che di madonna intende:
Diletti miei, or sofferite in pace,
Che vostra speme sia quanto mi piace
Là, ov'è alcun che perder lei s'attende.
E che dirà nell' Inferno a' malnati:
Io vidi la speranza de' beati.

Madonna è desiata in l'alto cielo—   [15–29]

[An Angel, of his blessed knowledge, saith
    To God: 'Lord, in the world that thou hast made
    A miracle in action is display'd
        By reason of a soul whose splendours fare
Even hither: and since Heaven requireth
    Nought saving her, for her it prayeth Thee,
    Thy Saints crying aloud continually.'
        Yet Pity still defends our earthly share
        In that sweet soul; God answering thus the prayer:
'My well beloved, suffer that in peace
    Your hope remain, while so My pleasure is,
    There where one dwells who dreads the loss of her,
And who in Hell unto the doom'd shall say,
"I have looked on that for which God's chosen pray."

My lady is desired in the high Heaven. . . .']

Rossetti's translation preserves something of the scholastic flavour
of the original—the angel's *divino intelletto,* the *meraviglia nell' atto,*
che procede da un anima, the Heaven, *che non have altro difetto che*
d'aver lei. Other features, such as the paronomasia in the reference
to Beatrice as *la speranza de' beati,* it misses.

Angels in fact are primarily Intellects or Intelligences. 'It is
in keeping with the order of the universe', Aquinas says,[19] 'for
the highest intellectual creature to be entirely intelligent, and not
in part, as in our soul. For this reason also the angels are called
intellects and *minds*'. As such, they are vitally involved in the

numerology which conveys part of the divine intention to the world below. It was assumed that the complicated but orderly movements of the celestial spheres were meaningful because they were physically controlled by angelic intelligences:

Voi che intendendo il terzo ciel movete

[You who *by understanding* move the third heaven.]

Dante begins his fifteenth *canzone*[20] (not included in the *Vita Nuova,* though related to it), and his use of *intendendo,* 'by understanding' illustrates his belief, not only that angelic control was intellectual, but that the angelic intellect had an object of understanding, namely the Providence of God, which it mediated through stellar and planetary motions in a way open to human cognisance at the highest level. The movements of the nine spheres reflect the nine-fold angelic hierarchy, which in turn reflects the Unity in Trinity, which is God.

Chapter XXIII describes the visionary Ascension, or perhaps rather Assumption, of Beatrice, accompanied by angels. Chapter XXVI is built round the prose passage:

This excellent lady, of whom I spoke in what hath gone before, came at last into such favour with all men, that when she passed anywhere folk ran to behold her; which thing was a deep joy to me: and when she drew near unto any, so much truth and simpleness (*onesta*) entered into his heart, that he dared neither to lift his eyes nor to return her salutation: and unto this, many who have felt it can bear witness. She went along crowned and clothed with humility, showing no whit of pride in all that she heard and saw: and when she had gone by, it was said of many, 'This is not a woman, but one of the beautiful angels of heaven', and there were some that said: 'This is surely a miracle; blessed be the Lord, who hath power to work thus marvellously.'

The word here translated 'miracle' is *meraviglia,* literally 'marvel', but in the sonnet which completes the chapter, this becomes *miracol:*

E par che sia una cosa venuta
Di cielo in terra a miràcol mostrare   [7–8]

[Seeming a creature sent from Heaven to stay
On earth, and show a miracle most sure.]

The word anticipates the passage from chapter XXX already
quoted: 'This lady was accompanied by the number nine to the
end that men might clearly perceive her to be a nine, that is, a
miracle (*un miracolo*), whose only root is the Holy Trinity'. The
earlier chapter establishes the link between the miracle and the
angelic orders.

In *Gli occhi dolenti per pietà del core* (chapter XXXII),
Beatrice is again associated with angels:

Ita n'è Beatrice in l'alto cielo
Nel reame ove gli angeli hanno pace,
E sta con loro.   [15–17]

[Beatrice is gone up into high Heaven,
The kingdom where the angels are at peace;
And lives with them . . .],

while in chapter XXXIV:

. . . il piacere della sua beltate
Partendo sè dalla nostra veduta,
Divenne spirital bellezza grande,
Che per lo cielo spande
Luce d'amor, che gli angeli saluta,
E lo intelletto loro alto e sottile
Face maravigliar; tanto è gentile!   [20–6]

Rossetti's translation is inadequate, and I give the prose version
from the Temple Classics edition:[21]

her winsome beauty withdrawing itself from our sight, became
a great spiritual loveliness, which through heaven sheds a light
of love, that saluteth the angels and maketh their high and rare
intelligence to marvel; so gentle it is!

Chapter XXXV tells how on the anniversary of her death

Dante occupied himself by 'drawing the resemblance of an angel upon certain tablets'. The sonnet which follows in chapter XXXVI concludes:

> O *nobile intelletto,*
> *Oggi fa l'anno che nel ciel salisti.*   [13–14]

> [O noble intellect!
> It is a year today that thou art gone.]

Intelletto speaks for itself. Rossetti says 'that thou art gone', but it should be noted that the Italian is more specific, meaning 'since you ascended to heaven', and that in the first of two commence/ ments of the sonnet given by Dante she is said to have ascended

> *Nel ciel dell' umiltate, ov è Maria,*   [5]

> [In the heaven of the humble (literally 'of humility'), where Mary is],

the empyrean heaven, that is paradoxically to say, beyond the spheres; the heaven of the humble, because in Mary God regarded the lowliness of his handmaiden. The Empyrean, how/ ever, is at the same time the home of the highest angelic orders, Cherubim, Seraphim and Dominations, with whom Beatrice is posthumously associated. The earlier emphasis on 6 may hint that in her earthly life she was associated with the 6 remaining orders, Thrones, Virtues, Principalities, Powers, Archangels and Angels, whose work is more closely associated with the universe contained by the celestial spheres.

The presence of Beatrice in the Empyrean is again empha/ sised in chapter XLI, where she is said now to look continually on the beautiful face of Jesus Christ, an office normally assumed by the three highest angelic orders. In the sonnet which concludes chapter XLII, the personified Sigh must pass the *primum mobile,* the outermost of the 9 spheres, before it can attain the presence of Beatrice in the Empyrean:

> *Oltre la spera, che più larga gira.*
> *Passa il sospiro ch'esce del mio core*   [1–2]

[Beyond the sphere which spreads to widest space
  Now soars the sigh that my heart sends above.]

The division which precedes this poem includes a reference to
Aristotle's *Metaphysics* [*IIa, cap.1*]:

> The spirit sees her such (that is, in such quality) that I cannot
> understand her; that is to say, my thought rises into the quality
> of her in a degree that my intellect cannot comprehend, seeing
> that our intellect [*il nostro intelletto*], is towards those blessed
> souls, like our eye weak against the sun; and thus the Philo-
> sopher says in the Second of the Metaphysics.

The same reference to Aristotle is made by the later poet Robert
Henryson (c.1420–c.1490) in one of his numerological poems,
The Preiching of the Swallow:[22]

> In *Metaphisik* Aristotell sayis
> That mannis saull is lyke ane bakkis ee,
> Quhilk lurkis still als lang as licht off day is,
> And in the gloming cummis furth to fle;
> Hir ene ar waik, the sone scho may not se.
>
> (*Fabillis* 1636–1640)

Both make the same point, that the imperfect human mind is
incapable of the angelic task of comprehending, or even visualis-
ing, the ultimate mysteries of the divinity. The ascended Beatrice
possesses these capabilities, which had been present even in her
mortal existence, and which were signified to the reader, not only
literally, by Dante's words, but mystically by the numerological
(purely intellectual and therefore angelic) structure of the work.

   'It might truly be said,' Émile Mâle remarked,[23] 'that there
was something of this sacred arithmetic in all the great works of
the Middle Ages.' His own illustration is the *Divina Commedia*,
which even more than the *Vita Nuova*:

> is built up on numbers. To the nine circles of Hell correspond
> the nine terraces of the mount of Purgatory and the nine heavens
> of Paradise. In that inspired poem nothing was left solely to
> inspiration. Dante determined that each part of his trilogy

should be divided into thirty-three cantos in honour of the thirty-three years of the life of Christ. [The *Inferno* has thirty-four cantos, but the first must be considered as a prologue.] In adopting the metrical form of the terzina he seems to have wished that the pre-eminently mystic number should enter into the very texture of his poem. . . . The most ardent imagination known in literature was also the most submissive. Dante accepted the law of numbers as a divine rhythm which the universe obeyed.

Subsequent work has only expanded and enriched these comments, which even in 1910 were commonplace of literary criticism.

Mâle does not note one of the most striking numerological features of the *Commedia*. The total number of cantos is 100, or, if one excludes the first as a prologue, 99. 100 and 99, together with 101, are the numbers which tend to appear whenever the subject of a literary work is the Otherworld or Eternity. In a decimal system of notation, 100 is the second limit of numbers, and like the first, 10, is the symbol of life beyond everyday mortal experience. One more—or one less—than the number shares the same quality—indeed, given the powers felt to inhere in 9 and 1, the presence of double 9 in the former and double 1 in the latter may actually have been felt to increase it. No numbers could have been more appropriate for the canto-tally of Dante's poem, which encompasses the entire range of Otherworldly experience, Hell, Purgatory and Paradise.

During the late fourteenth and early fifteenth centuries, a number of poems which exploit the same numerical convention were produced in the British Isles. One of these is Chaucer's *Parlement of Foulys*,[24] a vision of the Otherworld, which begins from the *Somnium Scipionis,* and continues with a dream vision of the garden ruled over by the goddesses Venus and Nature. The total number of stanzas may be variously calculated; most of the poem is composed in the seven-line rhyme-royal stanza, which Chaucer established in English and Scottish poetic usage, but at the very end there is a 'roundele', 13 lines long, which might, I suppose, be regarded as 1, 2, or 3 stanzas. In a way, it does not matter; the total is either 99, or 100, or 101, all of which have the same essential significance. I shall regard it as 99 in what follows.

The internal structure of the poem is highly patterned in a way which lies open to numerical analysis. The 7 chapters of *Somnium Scipionis* are summarised in 7 stanzas; the music of the 9 spheres is described in stanza 9; the assumed date of the actual parliament, February 14th, St Valentine's Day, is first men‑ tioned in stanza 45, which corresponds to February 14th, the 45th day of the New Year; in Chaucer's time as now popularly celebrated as beginning on January 1st.[25] The stanzas fall naturally into a pattern which emphasises 2, 6, with certain of its multiples and the factor 3, and 7, with certain of its multiples. Thus there is a prologue in 12 (2×6) stanzas, followed by the vision proper in 84 ($7 \times 2 \times 6$) stanzas, and the epilogue in 3 ($6/2$) stanzas. The vision, in turn, falls naturally into 2 sections, each of 42 (6×7) stanzas, (a), the description of the garden and its inhabitants, and (b), the actual parliament of birds. Within the description, 12 stanzas are devoted to the approach to the garden, 6 to the garden itself, 12 to the temple of Venus, and 12 to the description of Nature and the birds who attend her. The parliament breaks the pattern to a modest degree; 5 stanzas are devoted to Nature's speech, which opens the parliament (but the propriety of 5 in relation to Nature has been established earlier in this book); 36 (6×6) stanzas are devoted to the action of the parliament, and there is 1 concluding stanza.

Chaucer thus keeps to the rules of the game, but he is not, I feel, vitally concerned with numerological significance. His num‑ bers are decorative rather than functional: the main purpose seems to be no more than the preservation of symmetry in the narrative. The most interesting and elaborate British examples of literary numerology in the period come from areas well to the north and west of the metropolitan culture within which he flourished.

One example has already been quoted. At the beginning of this chapter I used *Sir Gawain and the Green Knight* to elucidate some of the numerology in the much earlier *Vie de Saint Alexis*. Another poem from the same area (the Derby / Cheshire / Lancashire borders), and perhaps by the same author, which makes an elaborate use of numerological techniques, is *Pearl*,[26] usually and inadequately described as an elegy on the death of the poet's daughter, the Pearl of the title. The poem is in fact an Otherworld dream-vision, experienced by the poet when in his grief he falls asleep on the grave of his infant daughter. He finds himself by a river, on the opposite bank of which stands a beautiful and magnificently clad child, in whom he recognises his lost daughter. She has become one of the 144,000 Brides of the Lamb, mentioned in *Revelation 14*. The dreamer has a long and puzzled conversation with her, which gives his grief some comfort, and he is eventually allowed to see the procession of the Brides of the Lamb with their consort in New Jerusalem itself. The city is also on the far bank of the stream. The sight fills him with such longing that he attempts to cross the water, an action which causes the vision to vanish, and he wakens to find himself once more in this world, a sadder man, but wiser in that he has gained some understanding of Christian salvation.

The figure 144,000 is obviously important for the poem, and equally obviously it is derived from *Revelation*, where as a multiple of 12 it forms part of the general numerological structure. *Pearl* is based on 101, the number of stanzas in the poem as a whole, 5, the number of stanzas included in each (save one) of the 20 sections which form the substructure of the poem, and 12, which at the lowest level is the number of lines in a single stanza. Section 15, where the 144,000 are first mentioned, contains 6 (12/2) rather than 5 stanzas. One reason for the total number of stanzas being 101 rather than 100 is that the number of lines thus becomes 1212—again emphasising 12, and also $12 \times 12 = 144$.

The numerological structure is further emphasised by the elaborate linkage, usually described by the Latin rhetorical term *concatenatio*, which unites stanza to stanza, section to section, beginning to end. The first line, 'Perle, plesaunte to prynces paye', returns in a slightly modified form as the last line, 'Ande precious perlez vnto his pay'. The last line of the first stanza, 'Of that pryuy perle wythouten spot', becomes a refrain concluding each stanza in the first section, and providing the introductory phrase for the first line of the second section, 'Fro spot my spyryt ther sprang in space' [*61*]. The last line of the first stanza of the second section then becomes a refrain for that section. The process is repeated, so that each section has a distinct identity, with the refrain of the final section more and more approximating to the first line of the poem. As a whole, the movement is circular.

In *Pearl,* circular movement and structure are identical, but that this need not always be so is shown by the *Kingis Quair,*[27] a poem usually attributed to James I of Scotland (1394–1437), and probably composed in the late 1420s. It purports to be based on James' experiences during the long captivity in England and France which followed his kidnap at sea by English pirates when he was ten years old. The first line of the first of its 197 rhyme-royal stanzas, 'Heigh in the hevennis figure circulere', is repeated as the last line of the 196th stanza, to be followed only by a single dedicatory verse. The repetition of the word 'circulere' confirms that the poet intended his work to be circular in the same sense as *Pearl.* He does not, however, here make use of 99, 100 or 101. Instead he makes use of 196, a perfect square ($14 \times 14 = 196$), and of 197, a prime number. James also draws a distinction between 'heaven', the Empyrean beyond the Primum Mobile, and 'the heavens', the 9 celestial spheres, as may be shown in stanza 196, where he distinguishes between 'him that hiest in the hevin sitt' (God), and 'the hevynnis figure circulere', the 9 celestial spheres. In such a context, it may not seem extravagant to suggest that the circular structure of the first 196 stanzas corresponds to that of the circular created universe, while the extra stanza, which transforms the perfect square to the prime, corresponds to the relationship between the unique Creator and his multiplex but orderly creation, an interpretation which agrees with James' idiosyncratic use of Boethius to illustrate relations, on the one hand between divine Providence which directly governs the movements of the stars and planets, and on the other, Fortune, the arbitrary mistress of affairs in the mortal world below.

The number 99 makes its appearance in the longest single episode of the poem, the dream vision of 3 goddesses, Venus, Minerva, and Fortune, who advise the imprisoned poet on the progress of his apparently hopeless love for the young woman whom he saw from his tower window as she disported herself in the garden below, and which occupies stanzas 74–172. The dreamer's experience here is decidedly extraterrestial; he is snatched up through the spheres until he reaches one of the zodiacal Houses of Venus [stanza 76]; later [stanza 124] he goes beyond the Primum Mobile to the palace of Minerva (Heavenly Wisdom) in the Empyrean, from which in stanza 151 he descends to the domain of Fortune—returns, that is to say, to Earth, Earth however in an archetypal and symbolic form, which is itself Otherworldly.

Within the dream vision, 50 stanzas are devoted to Venus and her court, 21 to the realm of Fortune, and (most significantly) 28, the second perfect number, to Minerva The 99 stanzas which represent otherworldly experience combine with the 13 stanzas of the prologue representing the thirteen spheres of the material universe which include 'the hevennis figure circulere' (Primum Mobile) together with Fixed Stars, seven Planets, Fire, Air, Water and Earth, the first group of 60 more or less autobiographical stanzas (60 minutes = 1 hour), and the second group of 24 (24 hours = 1 day), to make up the total of 196 stanzas in the circle. Distinctions are clearly and appropriately expressed.

James's method of combining the second limit of numbers with circular form thus differs from that of the *Pearl* poet or of Dante because, unlike theirs, his concern is not so much with the Otherworld as with this temporal creation, subjected to the whims of Fortune, but ultimately governed by a Boethian and benevolent Providence. His Otherworldly vision enables him to reconcile the benevolence with the apparent whimsicality, and his ultimate meaning is conveyed by the structure, which subordinates the vision to the circle squared in 196 stanzas, and transformed in 197.

5

The Renaissance and its Aftermath
Henryson — Spenser — Drummond — Milton

```
 1 2 3 4
  5 6 7
   8 9
    0
```

Although medieval numerological composition resulted from a fusion of biblical and classical (mainly Platonic) techniques and theories, the dominant element remained the biblical. Platonic influence, reinforced, no doubt, by the additional example of St Augustine, is present in the *Altus Prosator* and strong in Heiric's *Life* of Germanus; it is certainly present in the *Vita Nuova*. In all these works, however, the biblical is the predominant influence. The *Kingis Quair* is more secular, but cannot be described as especially Platonic. The emergence of a Platonic literature which was not necessarily derived only from the *Timaeus* and late antique echoes of other dialogues, belongs essentially to the later fifteenth century, with the earlier stages of its development governed by the vicissitudes of the Greek-speaking eastern Roman Empire, which the fall of Constantinople finally brought to an end in 1453. The diplomatic activities of the Byzantine court and church during the fourteenth and earlier fifteenth centuries brought to Italy such Greek scholars as Georgius Gemistus Plethon (c.1355–c.1450),[1] who had been preceded by his pupil, Manuel Chrysolaras (c.1350–1415),[2] described by F. W. Hall as 'the first competent teacher of Greek in Italy'. John Bessarion (c.1400–1472), who eventually became a cardinal of the western church, had also studied with Plethon, whom he accompanied to Florence for the church Council held there in 1438/9. Already almost a century earlier, Petrarch (1304–1374) had possessed Greek MSS, including one of Plato, but had struggled in vain with the intricacies of the language.[3] The full renaissance of western Platonism is marked by the foundation of the Florentine Academy in 1462, and by the translation of the dialogues into Latin undertaken by Marsilio Ficino (1433–1499), himself a Platonic philosopher of some distinction.[4]

Inevitably it was some time before a pure Platonism was the result; Ficino, for instance, interrupted his translation to produce a version of the writings attributed to Hermes Trismegistus, to which he accorded equal, or even superior, status, and whose tenets he incorporated in his own philosophy. Pico della Mirandola (1463–1494) added Cabbalistic elements, traces of which are readily visible in his posthumously published *Oratio*, usually known as 'On the Dignity of Man'.[5]

All this had an obvious potential effect on numerological composition. To quote Herschel Baker:[6]

> Ficino and Pico (and, across the Alps, Reuchlin) came to employ an erudite and fantastic numerology to demonstrate the correspondence between nature and spirit; and Bembo, in Castiglione's beautiful fourth book, described the facile progress from the experience of physical beauty to a rapturously mystical absorption into the Godhead. The temporal microcosm reflected the (mathematical) harmony and beauty of the spiritual macrocosm, and all experience merged into a continuum. Mystic and naturalist alike had learned to reverse the Nicene formula: they approached God through nature rather than nature through God.

Two centuries later, the Cambridge Platonists attempted much the same task, and the intervening period saw such important figures (often dabblers in natural magic) as Cornelius Agrippa (1486–1535), Paracelsus (1493–1541), Giordano Bruno (1549–1600), and Robert Fludd (1574–1637).

Hardin Craig rhetorically asked:

> What are we to think of the hundreds of earnest, patient, intelligent men—of Raymond Lully, Cornelius Agrippa, Paracelsus, Dr John Dee, and the great Cardan himself—

whose misfortune it was to devote their lives to false hypotheses?

The same question might well be asked of the writers discussed in this, and indeed in previous chapters, and the same answer found—the authority Agrippa thought he could draw from the Christianised Neoplatonic thought of St Augustine:

> For this is the harmony of the world that things supercelestial may be drawn down by the celestial, and supernatural by the natural, because there is one operative virtue which is diffused through all kinds of things, by which virtue, indeed, manifest things are produced out of occult causes.[8]

Craig added that this was the way in which the magician set to work, not necessarily setting himself against either Church or Faith. Agrippa, for instance, claimed[9] that his *De occulta Philosophia* (1531) contained nothing at variance with the laws of nature, or offensive to God, or injurious to religion:

> The virtues of the terrene orb proceed from no other cause than Celestial. Hence the Magician that will work by them, useth a cunning invocation of the superiors, with mysterious words, and a certain kind of ingenious speech, drawing the one to the other, yet by a natural force through a certain mutuall agreement betwixt them, whereby things follow of their own accord, or sometimes are drawn unwillingly. When we by the remembrance of its majesty being alwaies busied in Divine studies do every moment contemplate Divine things, by a sage and diligent inquisition, and by all degrees of creatures ascending even to the Archetype himself, [we] draw from Him the infallible vertue of all things, . . . the understanding of Divine things purgeth the mind from errors, and rendereth it Divine, giveth infallible power to our works, and driveth far the deceits and obstacles of all evil spirits, and together subjects them to our commands; yea it compels even good Angels and all the powers of the world unto our service.

The Neoplatonic numerological poet generally had more modest aims, but he had no reason to suppose that his precisely limned and proportioned verses, his 'certain kind of ingenious speech', were any less effective in procuring for his purposes the assistance of higher powers. If we limit ourselves to the authors discussed below, Spenser, I have little doubt, thought that by the composition of *Epithalamion* he ensured for his wife and himself a long and virtuous posterity; Henryson and Drummond that they were providing a means by which it was possible to attune oneself to supercelestial realities. Milton's diptych, *L'Allegro* and *Il Penseroso,* is not so much operative as dedicatory, but the dedication is to the service of a high mystery.

Although literary Neoplatonism of this kind is a European phenomenon, it will be seen that the present chapter deliberately limits itself to the old kingdoms of Scotland and England, before both were officially abolished in 1707. To the best of my knowledge, the first British vernacular poet to write fully within the tradition is Robert Henryson, whose *New Orpheus*[10] was probably composed during his association with the recently founded University of Glasgow, where he taught law, it seems probable, between 1462 and 1468.[11] His Platonism, still based essentially on the *Timaeus,* appears most obviously in the stanzas where he sets out the ratios and intervals which form the basis of medieval and renaissance musical theory:

Thar leirit he tonys proporcionate
As dupler, tripler and epitritus,
Hemiolius and eik the quadruplat,
Epogdous richt hard and curious;
And of thir sex, swet and delicious,
Richt consonant five hevinly symphonyis
Componit ar, as clerkis can devys.

First diatesseroun, full sweit, I wis,
And diapasoun, symple and duplate,
And diapente, componit with a dis;
Thir makis five, of thre multiplicat.   [31 – 2.226 – 36]

In these the reader will recognise the components of the Platonic *Anima Mundi,* or Soul of the World discussed in chapter two of the present work. Henryson too knew the source on which he was drawing:[12]

> Quhilk ermony throw all this mappamond,
> Quhill moving ces, unite perpetuall,
> Of this quik World Plato the Saull can call.
>
> [*30.223–5*]

As noted in chapter two, the Soul of the World is formulated in the numerical series which begins from unity and runs through the first even and first odd numbers together with their squares and cubes. The final number of the sequence is 27. Henryson's description is completed in the 27th 7-line stanza of his poem (the sequence is deliberately broken after the 19th stanza by the intrusion of 5 lyrical 10-line stanzas). 27 is not only the cube of 3, it is also the sum of all the other numbers in the series, and so in a sense contains the remainder of the formula, which, it should be noted, applies to the individual human soul as much as it does to the animating power present in the divine creation.

Henryson emphasises[13] that tropologically Orpheus and his wife Eurydice, the two main characters of the poem, are allegories of the human soul in two contrasting aspects. Orpheus is the intellectual, Eurydice, the appetitive. The appetitive is snared by sensuality and falls from heaven; in search of her, the intellectual power descends towards incarnation through the spheres of the stars and planets, but finds no trace of his mate. The music created by the movements of the spheres, however, based as it is on the ratios and intervals which Henryson lists, constitutes the unfallen Soul of the World, which has the ability to regenerate the 'music', that is the intellectual power, of Orpheus, and so prepare him to undertake the rescue of Eurydice from the powers of incarnation, primarily represented by Pluto and Proserpine, King and Queen of Hell. His ultimate lack of success results, not from any failure on the part of the Soul of the World, but from the inherent limitations of intellect unaided by grace. Orpheus begins his descent, not from earth, but from the native regions of the soul beyond the Primum Mobile or *aplanes*.

The entire poem consists of 57 stanzas, 52 of which are in 7-line rhyme-royal, while the remaining 5 [stanzas 20–4] are in an elaborate 10-line lyric form. As I have noted, this last is intruded into the main sequence after the 19th stanza, at the point, that is to say, at which the formulaic sequence has reached 9, the first masculine square ($1+2+3+4+9=19$). 8, the first feminine cube is still required to make up 27, the first masculine cube. The ratio 9/8 is dissonant, and is excluded by Henryson from his list of 'symphonies'. The position of the intruded sequence is thus appropriate for stanzas expressing the disruption of the unified human soul at birth, and their number, 5, is presumably to be taken as representing the five senses, through which the disruption has taken place. The fall of Eurydice is the result of sensuality, and Hell, where she is afterwards to be found, is the realm of uncontrolled bodily appetites produced by the shock of sensual experience. Hell itself, the realm of this experience, is appropriately emblematised by the final 25 (5×5) stanzas.

The first 27 stanzas, excluding the lyrical outburst, correspondingly represent the rationality of the Soul of the World. The total of 52 7-line stanzas also corresponds, however, to the 52 7-day weeks of the solar year. The movement of the Sun through the signs of the Zodiac, completed in a year, brings us back to the Soul of the World by way of the music of the spheres.

The 7-line stanzas thus in a sense represent the circle of the calendar year. Line 93, where Eurydice is described as walking forth 'in till a Maii mornyng', may be taken to represent May 1st, and the summer solstice, regarded as having an ideal position, June 15th, the middle day of the middle month of the year, is represented by line 138 of the narrative, line 188 of the entire poem, the point at which Orpheus enters Watling Street, the Milky Way, and so begins his descent through the spheres. The summer solstice in the zodiacal constellation Cancer, was regarded by Neoplatonists as the portal through which human souls on their path to incarnation entered the material universe. It was the portal of men. December 15th, the winter solstice in Capricorn, was known as the portal of gods, because this was the route by which perfected souls eventually returned to their rightful abode of immortality, to be reckoned among the gods.[14] In the poem this is represented by line 369, the middle line of the stanza in which the music of Orpheus gains a conditional remission for Eurydice:

> Than Orpheus before Pluto sat doun,
> And in his handis quhite his harp can ta,
> And playit mony suete proporcion,
> With base tonys in Hypodoria,
> With gemilling in Hyperlydia;
> Til at the last for reuth and grete pitee
> Thay wepit sore that coud hym here and see.
>
> [51.366-72]

It is notable that at this point the technical vocabulary of musical theory reappears. Hypodoria and Hyperlydia were the lowest and highest of the fifteen classical Tonoi or Keys, and in terms of the music of the spheres correspond to the Moon, the lowest, and the Fixed Stars, the highest.[15] The choice of these *tonoi* implies that Orpheus in his playing utilised the full range, and so by producing a 'proporcioun' which corresponds to the music of the spheres and the Soul of the World, gave Eurydice and himself the opportunity to return from the world of incarnation to the Elysian Fields by way of the portal of the gods. They fail because Orpheus looks back towards the realm of sensuality. The narrative appropriately ends with a complaint against the bitter-sweet earthly love which caused their tragedy:

> Quhat art thou lufe? How sall I the dyffyne?
> Bitter and suete, cruel and merciable.   [56.401-2]

It would be wrong to say that Henryson in this poem was completely unaffected by the biblical tradition. No fifteenth-century poet could be. His work, however, with its emphasis on incarnation, is more thoroughly suffused with Platonism than is that of any earlier vernacular poet. In this he belongs to the Renaissance rather than to the late Middle Ages.

The closest parallel to Henryson's allegorical narrative is to be found in a poem written more than a century later by Edmund Spenser (?1552–1599), *An Hymne in Honour of Beautie,* first published in 1596 as one of *Fowre Hymnes.*[16] Spenser identifies ultimate Beauty with the pattern used by the Platonic Demiurge to create the universe, the influence of which, felt by every earthly thing, is experienced in its greatest intensity by human lovers, who find complete satisfaction only after death, when the soul returns to its native place in, or by way of, the Sun. In their previous descent to incarnation, they have gained from the Sun a portion of its light, which corresponds to ultimate Beauty and remains with them beautifying the body and enabling the soul to recognise light from the same source partly concealed within the body of others. The descent is made, however, not from the Sun, but from beyond the spheres, at a time when the Sun's position in the Zodiac is appropriate. Spenser's words are not specific, but the underlying reference to the portal of men and portal of gods is as clear as in Henryson:

> But that faire lampe, from whose celestiall ray
> That light proceedes, which kindleth lovers fire,
> Shall never be extinguisht nor decay,
> But when the vitall spirits doe expyre,
> Unto her native planet shall retyre,
> For it is heavenly borne and can not die,
> Being a parcell of the purest skie.
>
> For when the soule, the which derived was
> At first, out of that great immortall Spright,
> By whom all live to love, whilome did pas
> Downe from the top of purest heavens hight,
> To be embodied here, it then tooke light
> And lively spirits from that fayrest starre,
> Which lights the world forth from his firie carre.
>
> [15–16.99–112]

Spenser's Platonic orthodoxy is a little suspect here: it was normally held that in the sphere of the Sun the descending soul

found sense-perception and imagination:[17] his other references—
to the essential identity of the individual human soul with the
Soul of the World, the descent and return of the soul—are more
easily fitted into the general Platonic context, and are also easily
parallelled in Henryson's poem, although it is perhaps somewhat
surprising that Spenser does not mention the music of the
spheres.

   Fowre Hymnes includes tantalising hints of numerological
structure which, in common with others,[18] I have not been able
to decipher to my own satisfaction. Spenser, however, is a figure
of great importance in the history of the mode. Two of the most
influential books written in the last three decades have been
devoted to his work. I refer, of course, to *Short Time's Endless
Monument,* by A. Kent Hieatt, published in 1960, and to *Spenser
and the Numbers of Time,* by Alastair Fowler, published in 1964.
The first deals with *Epithalamion,* first published with *Amoretti* in
1595, the second with *The Faerie Queene,* the first three books of
which were published in 1590, the second three in 1596.
(Spenser's intention was to compose a first total of 12 books, and
the poem, as we have it, is therefore incomplete.) To a considerable extent, modern interest in numerological criticism, at least
in the context of English literature, takes its origin from these two
works.

   The starting point of Hieatt's book is the observation that
Epithalamion contains, if we include the Envoy, 24 stanzas, 365
long and 68 short lines. 'If we exclude the Envoy' [I quote the
late Miss Enid Welsford]:[19]

> the marriage ode contains 23 stanzas, each consisting of groups
> of long lines—pentameters and a concluding hexameter—
> divided (with two exceptions) by 3 short lines, which (again
> with the two exceptions) are trimeters. Stanzas 15 and 23
> contain only 2 short lines: the number of long lines contained
> in the 23 stanzas varies from 15 to 16; consequently these
> stanzas vary in length from 17 to 19 lines. The Envoy consists
> of 6 pentameters and one tetrameter.

   This structure is to be interpreted in terms which bear some relationship to those found applicable to many earlier poems. Professor Hieatt has indicated that *Epithalamion* is in a sense circular, a feature, I may add, best brought out by the two forms of the refrain, which in the first 16 stanzas is positive—variations on 'That all the woods may answer and your eccho ring'—and in the following 7 is negative—variations on 'The woods no more shal answere, nor your echo ring'. The change corresponds to the movement from day to night in the course of events narrated in the poem, and is indicated at the beginning of stanza 17:

> Now ceasse ye damsels your delights forepast;
> Enough is it, that all the day was youres:
> Now day is doen, and night is nighing fast.   [17.296–8]

The division of the poem into day- and night-stanzas indicates that the total 24 corresponds to the 24 hours of the day, which in turn is 'Barnaby the bright', June 11th. In Spenser's time this coincided with the summer solstice (and incidentally with the 'portal of men'). The ratio 16/8 approximately corresponds to the ratio of the hours of day to those of night in southern Irish latitudes at this time of year. But if each stanza corresponds to a sidereal hour (the type of hour, that is to say, which clocks record), the poem begins and ends at the same hour on two successive days. In this way at least, the form of the poem is circular.

The 365 long lines strongly suggest that the circle is not merely that of the day, but also of the year. The 68 additional short lines offer some difficulty, a difficulty which Hieatt ingeniously solved by regarding them as marking both the quarter hours of the day, and the sum of the units which make up the year—4 seasons + 12 months + 52 weeks = 68. But here there is another difficulty. 96 quarter hours make up 24 hours—to divide a stanza representing a single hour into quarter hours 3 short lines would be necessary. The poem as a whole would then contain 72 short lines, whereas, as has been seen, it contains only 68. Hieatt suggests[20] that, with the quarter hours, we have, not absolute consistency, but a 'dominant auditory image', repeated with sufficient frequency to have its effect. This would seem to imply that the precision with which Spenser gives the units whose sum makes up the year is of great importance. It is difficult however to see in what sense this is so. I suggest with some diffidence that 365 is the important figure. Even within the system suggested by Professor Hieatt, not all long lines are of the same length; the majority are pentameters, but the refrains hexa-meters. Usually the short lines rhyme with the immediately preceding long line, as in:

> This day the sunne is in his chiefest hight
> With Barnaby the bright.   [*15.265–6*]

If long and short line are taken together as a single unit with internal rhyme, the line-count is then 365, a more elegant pro-cedure, which at the same time simplifies problems of inter-pretation.

In Hieatt's exposition, the 6 long lines of the *Envoi* corres-pond to the retardation of the movement of the Sun by com-parison with that of the heaven in the course of the year. The heaven returns to its initial position in 359 days; the Sun however requires a further 6 to catch up.

As has been said, the poem celebrates the events of a single notable day, that of the poet's wedding, which numerologically and otherwise is seen in a wider and longer perspective, without lessening its individual significance. On the marriage day the Sun stood at the portal of men, through which souls came to incarnation. Correspondingly and appropriately, the night-stanzas concern themselves with generation and procreation:

> But let the night be calme and quietsome,
> Without tempestuous storms or sad afray:
> Lyke as when Ioue with fayre Alcmena lay,
> When he begot the great Tirynthian groome:
> Or lyke as when he with thy selfe did lie,
> And begot Maiesty.   [*18.326–31*]

The final emphasis is on the possible progeny of the night itself:

Poure out your blessing on vs plentiously,
And happy influence vpon vs raine,
That we may raise a large posterity,
Which from the earth, which they may long possesse,
With lasting happinesse,
Vp to your haughty pallaces may mount,
And for the guerdon of theyr glorious merit
May heauenly tabernacles there inherit,
Of blessed Saints for to increase the count.
So let vs rest, sweet loue, in hope of this.

[23.415-24]

The final emphasis, it will be noted, is not on the world of days and years, but on eternity, the world beyond the *aplanes,* and the home to which enlightened incarnate spirits eventually return.

To say this is to bring out at once Spenser's Platonism, and his kinship with earlier poets who had used circular form as a symbol of eternity– the Pearl poet, James 1, and in a more immediately Platonic and less optimistic way, Robert Henryson. Professor Hieatt's conclusion[21] is rather different:

We must think of the substance of the poem as the substance of time itself—duration with its divisions—and we must see a year as a day, as God does. Finally we must see how man and the universe mirror each other, and what paradoxical boon is granted to all of us: that though we may not endure individually, our mortality and the insufficiency of all created things is, by grace, only one aspect of a total situation of which cyclical return is the other face, until such time as time shall cease [80-1].

This approach is based on the analogy of the elegiac Mutabilitie cantos of *The Faerie Queene,* published posthumously in 1609:[22]

Then gin I thinke on that which Nature sayd,
Of that same time when no more *Change* shall be,
But stedfast rest of all things firmely stayd
Vpon the pillours of Eternity,
That is contrayr to *Mutabilitie*:

For, all that moueth, doth in *Change* delight:
But thence forth all shall rest eternally
With Him that is the God of Sabbaoth hight:
O that great Sabbaoth God, graunt me that Sabaoths sight.
                                                          [*8.2*]

But *Epithalamion* is not an elegy; it is a celebration, and the emphasis is not 'until such time as time shall cease', but on rest and hope. The poem itself in terms of time will be an endless monument: this is the customary boast of the Renaissance poet. The line also means however that the poem has celebrated the chief achievement of time in the production of blessed souls who will finally be independent of itself. But the poem cannot move outside time, as can the human souls who are its subject, and it is on them that in stanza 23 the emphasis falls. The song is a temporal ornament; the souls are immortal, and in addition have the physical capacity to beget or bear other souls, equally immortal.

      As it did with the *Divina Commedia,* space prevents me from giving any extended treatment of *The Faerie Queene.* The main point of Professor Fowler's rich and rewarding book is, however, that the poem must be regarded numerologically in two ways. In part one he analyses the six completed books individually in terms of the monad, the dyad, the triad, the tetrad, the pentad and the hexad, terms which are familiar from Heiric's *Life* of Germanus. In the second part he attempts rather less successfully to relate the same books, together with the Mutability cantos, to the planetary week. Book *1* belongs to the Sun, Book *2* to the Moon, Book *3* to Minerva and Venus, Book *4* to Mercury and Venus, Book *5* to Jupiter, Book *6* to Venus and the Mutabilitie cantos to Saturn. Many of the points which Fowler makes in this part are convincing, but the overall scheme is rather less so. Apart from anything else, it is obviously difficult to relate such an analysis in terms of 7 books to an uncompleted poem intended to contain 12. Part *3* is an attempt to formulate a theory of numerological criticism. Fowler bases his work on line and stanza totals, and on character groups within the separate books and the poem as a whole, all seen against the vast background of Renaissance and earlier writings on numerology and mythology. It is safe to say that his book has reshaped every reader's way of approaching Spenser—I may say, to the general advantage.

———————

One of the biblical texts which helped towards a fusion of Greek with Hebrew ideas in numerological composition has already been quoted in chapter one. It is the apocryphal *Wisdom of Solomon 11.20,* 'But thou hast ordered all things by measure and number and weight'. Curtius quotes examples of its use in medieval Latin,[23] and in the vernaculars one might refer to the prologue of Henryson's *The Preiching of the Swallow,*[24] where it occurs at a significant point, marking the presence in the poem of numerological structures. The text is similarly quoted by William Drummond of Hawthornden (1585-1649) in his *An Hymne of the Fairest Faire,*[25] which forms part of the sequence entitled *Flowres of Sion* (1623). The quotation comes from the account of Love and Justice as attributes of God:

> By this [Love] thou brought this engine great to light,
> By that [Justice] it flamed in number, measure, weight.
>
> [85–6]

The emphasis in Henryson—'In number, weeht and dew proportioun' [8.53]—is on proportion; in Drummond, however, it is on 'weight', the word which occurs in final rhyming position. The subject of the poem is the 'Engine great' of the universe, powered by the Trinity, the Fairest Faire of the title. To correspond with the quotation, the numerology has as its basis a unit of weight. The entire poem consists of 336 lines. 336 divided by the 3 of the Trinity gives 112, the numerical equivalent of the hundredweight, which contains 112 lbs. The poem consists of 3 hundredweights, corresponding to God in 3 Persons.

The first hundredweight, the first 112 lines, is essentially concerned with God the Father, and ends with the significant line applied to him, 'Midst, end, beginning, where all good doth pause' [*112*]. The second hundredweight begins with the begetting in Eternity of God the Son:

> Hence of thy Substance, differing in nought,
> Thou in Eternitie thy Sonne foorth brought.   [*113–14*]

The Son does not, however, occupy the whole of the second hundredweight: together with the Holy Ghost, he occupies a total of 33 lines [*114–46*], brief, but numerologically meaningful in terms of the belief, already often mentioned, that Christ was crucified when he was 33 years old. The Crucifixion was followed by the descent at Pentecost of the Holy Ghost.

The remainder of the second hundredweight moves in a somewhat different direction; it is occupied by the angelic orders, the figure of Nature, and that part of the province assigned to her which is occupied by the stars and the planets from Saturn to the Sun. As will be shown, the reason for this is that the second hundredweight overlaps with another subdivision, indicated by the subtitle of the poem, 'An Hymn of the Nature, Attributes, and Works of God', that between uncreated being (the nature and attributes of God), and created being (the works of God), a division which occurs, after a transitional passage, at line 162.

The third hundredweight opens with a Hermetic and Copernican[26] passage on the pre-eminent and creative role of the sun in the material universe:

> Heart of this All, of what is knowne to Sence,
> The likest to his Makers Excellence,
> In whose diurnall motion doth appeare
> A Shadow, no, true pourtrait of the yeare.   [*225–8*]

By implication the Sun resembles his maker as the day resembles the year—perhaps also the Platonic or Great Year, which is to form the history of the universe and complete the circle of time. But this is not the only implication; the reader should also bear in mind the sun-like appearance of the Holy Ghost in tongues like flames of fire at the third hour of the first Pentecost [*Acts, 2.3*], and recognise in the phrase 'faire life-giving Source' [*223*], which introduces the lines quoted, an echo of the Nicene Creed,

'And I believe in the Holy Ghost, the Lord, the Giver of life'. The continuing belief that the lower world is the sphere in which the Holy Ghost, like the Sun, is predominantly active is indicated by the conclusion of a sonnet written more than two centuries later by Gerard Manley Hopkins:

Because the Holy Ghost over the bent
World broods with warm breast, and with, ah, bright wings.
[*God's Grandeur, 13–14*]

The end of the third hundredweight returns to the first Person of the Trinity, the three hundredweight thus moving Neoplatonically from God, by way of God, back again to God.

The division into hundredweights takes us some way towards understanding the structure, but to gain a more complete understanding, it is necessary to return to the distinction between uncreated and created being which, as has been noted, occurs at line 162. The Trinity and its 13 Attributes occupy the preceding lines. The poem is thus divided when it has completed 162/336ths of its course. To appreciate the significance, it is necessary to divide both dividend and divisor by 3, an appropriately triadic and trinitarian process, and to regard the ratio as 54/112. The sum of the numbers which constitute the Lambda formula for the Soul of the World ($1+2+3+4+9+8+27$) is 54, the new dividend. 112, the divisor, is, as has been seen, the hundredweight, the basic unit of measurement within the poem. The nature and attributes of God bears the same numerological relationship to the poem as a whole that the Soul of the World does to the Platonic cosmos, or the human soul to the human body.

The final 174 lines [*163–336*] thus represent the body of the cosmos in that they deal with created being. The chief characteristic of that body is that it exists in time. Of the 174 lines, the last 52 [*285–336*] show the total dependence of this body on God the Father. The first 18 [*163–80*] deal with the 9 orders of angels, $18 = 9 \times 2$, with the multiplier representing the dignity of the angels, while remaining less than the triple figure used to represent the Trinity. 156 (3×52) lines are thus devoted to creation below the angels, a Trinitarian representation of the year, perhaps the Platonic or Great Year already mentioned. To this the Persons of the Trinity are related in reverse order, culminating in the final return to the Father.

Lines 181–232 deal with the stars and planets, including the Sun and Moon, the music of whose movements corresponds to the Holy Ghost as Soul of the World. 6 [181–6] of the 52 lines, corresponding to the six days of Creation, are devoted to Nature; 16 lines [187–202] to the Stars, reflecting in the multiplier their greater dignity by comparison with Earth and the seven planetary spheres; 30 lines [203–32] to the seven Planets, corresponding to the 30-year orbit of Saturn, the outermost planet, and the 30-day synodic month of the innermost, the Moon.

Lines 233–84 are devoted to Man as a prisoner on Earth, the lowest depth of creation, whose dignity, originally in itself, now by virtue of its redemption by the second Person of the Trinity, is nevertheless greater than that of all the remainder.

The final 52 lines [285–336] deal, as has been noted, with the relation of the first Person, God the Father, to the lower creation.

Drummond's poem is eclectic, based, as it is, on Ronsard's *Hymne de l'Eternité,* on Spenser's *An Hymne of Heavenly Beautie,* and on sonnet XXVI of Sidney's *Astrophel and Stella*[27]—to name no others. In none of these, however, is to be found a parallel complex use of numerological techniques. The prayer near the beginning of the poem, which hints at a cosmic numerological structure:

> Grant mee (Times Father, world-containing King)
> A Pow'r, of Thee in pow'rfull Layes to sing,
> That as thy Beautie in Earth lives, Heaven shines,
> So it may dawne, or shadow in my Lines.   [13–16]

is more than answered by the verses which follow. No better example of the imitation which is also renewal could be found.

Numerological symbolism is to be found in the works of Milton (1608–74) and Dryden (1631–1700), but it is perhaps fair to comment that in them, and in their contemporaries, it has lost something of the imaginative intensity characteristic of the earlier writers discussed in this book. The change substantially reflects a change in mental attitudes towards the universe, introduced to western Europe by the work of the astronomers Copernicus (1473–1543), Galileo (1564–1642), and Kepler (1571–1630), and by that of the philosophers Bacon (1561–1626), Descartes (1596–1650) and Locke (1632–1704). There was a pervasive loss of faith in the traditional pattern of the universe, a loss which can be as well illustrated from *Paradise Lost* (1667) as from the *Principia* (1687) of Newton or Locke's *Essay concerning Human Understanding* (1690):

> Whether the Sun predominant in Heav'n
> Rise on the Earth, or Earth rise on the Sun,
> Hee from the East his flaming road begin,
> Or Shee from West her silent course advance
> With inoffensive pace that spinning sleeps
> On her soft axle, while she paces Ev'n,
> And bears thee soft with the smooth Air along,
> Solicit not thy thought with matters hid,
> Leave them to God above, him serve and fear.
>
> (*Paradise Lost*,[28] VIII.160–8)

The greater space given to the second alternative strongly suggests that Milton accepted a heliocentric view of the universe, a view more difficult than earlier ones to express in terms of literary numerology. In fact, the first traces of this attitude are to be found in Drummond,[29] but they did not particularly inhibit him in the composition of *An Hymne of the Fairest Faire*. For later poets, numerology became in some sense a game—a game which might be skilfully played, but which in the end was more an adornment than an essential part of the intellectual life. Eventually it became a lie, at which point such numerology disappears from poetry.

The publication of *Paradise Lost* in 1667 was separated from that of his early *Poems* (1645) by a gap of more than twenty years. It is not therefore surprising that more convincing evidence has been found for the presence of numerology in the earlier than in the later poems. The most significant point demonstrated[30] about *Paradise Lost* is that its exact centre is Christ's ascent of his chariot during the war in heaven:

> Hee in Celestial Panoply all arm'd
> Of radiant *Urim,* work divinely wrought,
> Ascended, at his right hand Victory
> Sat Eagle-wing'd.   [VI.760–3]

This is striking enough and important, but much richer results have been obtained for the early poems—Maren-Sofie Rostvig's article, for instance, 'Elaborate song: conceptual structure in Milton's *On the Morning of Christ's Nativity*',[31] and Alastair Fowler's 'To Shepherd's ear: the form of Milton's *Lycidas*'.[32]

I propose to conclude this chapter with an analysis of *L'Allegro* and *Il Penseroso,* the companion pieces which Milton wrote, probably towards the end of his time at Cambridge, and which were published together in 1645. Together they contain a total of 328 lines, a figure which represents the number of days in the sidereal year of the Moon—the time, that is to say, required by the Moon to complete 12 circuits of the Zodiac. 328 represents an exact period of 327.85992 days, 12 times the sidereal month of 27.32166 days. This figure differs from that of 29.53059 days, the synodic month, because it is unrelated to the apparent move-ments of the Sun—a point which corresponds to the total effect of the two poems and reflects relations between them. In lunar terms, however, the Sun is not totally ignored. The synodic year is 354.36708 days, a number which in literature is usually treated as 354. It will be noted that 176, the number of lines in *Il Penseroso,* comes as close as is possible for a poem composed in regular rhyming couplets, to half that number. Both 'years' are thus represented.

It should be added that if we subtract from the line total of *Il Penseroso,* first the 10 introductory lines dismissing 'vain deluding joys', secondly, the final couplet, both of which are exactly paralleled in *L'Allegro,* we are left with a line total of 164, exactly half of 328, the sidereal year of the Moon. The lines subtracted may be added to the 152 of *L'Allegro,* when the total again becomes 164.

Noticeably, while the Moon is nowhere named in *L'Allegro,* it occupies a prominent position in *Il Penseroso,* where in a single passage it is twice mentioned, once in association with the nightingale, once not. The first refers to the summer, the second to the winter moon, thus emphasising the circuit of the lunar year. The passage occupies 14 lines, which conventionally represent the period from new to full moon, half a sidereal month. In both references the moon is to be regarded as full:

> While *Cynthia* checks her Dragon yoke,
> Gently o'er th'accustom'd Oak;
> Sweet Bird that shunn'st the noise of folly,
> Most musical, most melancholy!
> Thee Chantress oft the Woods among,
> I woo to hear thy Even-Song;
> And missing thee, I walk unseen
> On the dry smooth-shaven Green,
> To behold the wand'ring Moon,
> Riding near her highest noon,
> Like one that had been led astray
> Through the Heav'n's wide pathless way.
> And oft, as if her head she bow'd,
> Stooping through a fleecy cloud.   [59–72]

The words are pictorially evocative, but at the same time they are intellectually precise. In medieval terms, the Moon is a planet, a word which etymologically means 'wanderer', and which was used because the planets, unlike the 'fixed' stars, 'wandered', moved, that is to say, through and round the Zodiac. They were defined by a relationship not to the Sun, but to the stars. The Sun was itself a planet. At any given moment the movement might appear random, but over longer periods a system would appear in terms of which the movements were regular and predictable. Paradoxically therefore the adjective 'wandering', applied to the Moon, and afterwards expanded in the couplet:

Like one that had been led astray
Through the Heav'n's wide pathless way.   [*69–70*]

means precisely the reverse of what it seems to say, and contains
another reference to the lunar year.

Paradox is also present in the application to the Moon of the
distinctively solar word 'noon' (67). There is no daily lunar
equivalent of the solar noon: Milton applies the term, however, to
full moon, which as a consequence of the movement of the Earth
round the Sun occurs successively in the different signs of the
Zodiac during the 12 sidereal months of the lunar year. Because
the full moon is separated from the sun by an angle of 180 degrees,
the signs which in solar terms belong to summer are winter signs
for the moon, and vice versa. The lunar 'highest noon' in Cancer
thus occurs at a time when the sun is at the furthest point south
in Capricorn—midwinter, that is to say, in terms of the northern
hemisphere. Again the lunar year receives emphasis.

Il Penseroso is 24 lines longer than *L'Allegro*. The figure
emphasises time, the 24 hours of the solar day. Both poems are
substantially ordered in terms of a day, which in *L'Allegro* begins
with morning, with evening in *Il Penseroso*. *L'Allegro,* the day
poem, is one of brightness, noise and bustle, *Il Penseroso* of dark-
ness and a silence which is sometimes enhanced by music. The
effect of its greater length, and later position in the sequence, is to
give it the greater authority; the reader in effect is urged to accept
thoughtful and learned melancholy rather than a cheerfulness
which in the last analysis is somewhat vapid.

The point is numerologically accented. The mid-point, the
highest noon of the poems taken together, which occupies lines
12 and 13 of *Il Penseroso,* is the invocation of Melancholy in the
second poem:

Hail divinest Melancholy,
Whose Saintly visage is too bright.

'Divinest' and 'Saintly' are powerful adjectives anywhere in
Milton's work and it should be noted that Melancholy is black
(etymologically and in contemporary physiological and psycho-

logical theory) only because she possesses a divine or saintly excess of light.

If *L'Allegro* is itself halved in the same way, the result has no significance. Not so with *Il Penseroso,* where the mid-way point occupies the couplet:

> With thrice great *Hermes,* or unsphere
> The spirit of *Plato* to unfold—   [88-9]

The importance of Plato has often been emphasised in this book and in this chapter. Hermes Trismegistus, the supposed Egyptian contemporary of Moses, was almost as important, and although Casaubon had demonstrated[33] some years before Milton wrote his poem that the Hermetic writings were in fact productions of the early Christian era, much influenced by various kinds of Neoplatonism and Gnosticism, Milton—at least in his *persona* of Il Penseroso—obviously still regarded them as very ancient works, the actual ultimate source of the Platonic doctrines.

Hermetic philosophy was particularly associated with silence,[34] and is therefore fittingly associated with a poem which so much emphasises that quality. It is also much concerned with the power exercised by the adept over daemons—not the evil and mischievous figures suggested by present-day associations of the word, but intermediate powers residing in the elements, and having a mysterious sympathy with the world-ruling planets:

> And of these *Daemons* that are found
> In fire, air, flood, or underground,
> Whose power hath a true consent
> With Planet, or with Element.   [93-6]

The theme of daemonic sympathy returns in the prayer which concludes the poem:

> And may at last my weary age
> Find out the peaceful hermitage,
> The Hairy Gown and Mossy Cell,
> Where I may sit and rightly spell
> Of every Star that Heav'n doth shew,
> And every Herb that sips the dew.

Some of the Hermetic writings magically linked the Moon, the presiding divinity of the two poems, and her fellow-planets, directly to the fabric of this world below.[35]

The passage about the two philosophers is linked to the movement of time, and the relationship of time to eternity, first by the fact that it is 12 lines long, a figure obviously associated with the twice-twelve hours of the day, but, as was demonstrated in chapter 1, also used biblically to denote eternity. Much the same is true of the reference to the constellation of the Great or Little Bear, *Ursa Major* or *Minor*:

> Or let my Lamp at midnight hour,
> Be seen in some high lonely Tow'r,
> Where I may oft outwatch the *Bear,*
> With thrice great *Hermes*—   [85–8]

Midnight and stellar revolutions are marks of the passage of time, but because neither Arctic constellation ever sets, but in the northern hemisphere is visible at night throughout the year moving round the celestial pole, they became for Hermeticists a symbol of eternal energy.[36]

Plato himself is pre-eminently the philosopher of eternity, and as such is called up by the poet:

> to unfold
> What Worlds, or what vast Regions hold
> The immortal mind that hath forsook
> Her mansion in this fleshly nook.   [88–92]

Milton here is referring primarily to the vision of Er in the *Republic,* to the myth of the *Phaedrus,* and to that of the *Phaedo.*[37]

The Moon, the lowest of the planets, is often associated with Saturn, the highest. Saturn in *Il Penseroso* is the incestuous but guiltless father of Melancholy by his daughter Vesta, goddess of the hearth. This parentage twice receives numerological emphasis. Saturn is often etymologically identified with Father Time, because his Greek name, Kronos, closely resembles the Greek word for 'time', *chronos.* In Latin too it was possible to make such specious etymologies as that of Isidore;[38] he is called

Saturn, *quod saturetur annis,* 'because he is saturated with years'. Isidore goes on to equate him with time. The slow movement of the planet Saturn, which requires 30 years to complete its orbit of the Zodiac, also contributed to this identification. Both factors are present in *Il Penseroso*. Saturn is first mentioned in line *24,* and the genealogy of Melancholy is completed in line *30* with an account of the secret assignations made by Saturn with Vesta which led to the birth of their child.

The sequence of the poem is made up partly of round-number units of 10 and 20 lines, partly of units, the significance of which is to be seen in terms of the Moon or the 24-hour day. The first is the 10-line prologue in which bastard joys are dismissed; this is followed by the 20 lines in which Melancholy is described and her genealogy given. The invocation occupies 28 lines [*31–58*], a number which represents the number of days in a sidereal month, and at the same time is the second perfect number. This is followed by the 14 lines [*59–72*] in which the summer and winter full moons, 14 days old, are described. 12 lines [*73–84*] begin with the sound of the curfew, and end with the crying of the night-hours by the bellman. The passage of time is thus emphasised, combined with details—the glow of embers and the sound of the cricket—which link Melancholy to her parent, Vesta, goddess of the sacred hearth. It is by the numinous quality of such details that Milton strengthens the suggestion of time mingling with eternity already present in the number 12, and further emphasised in the following group of 12 lines [*85–96*], already discussed, centred on Hermes Trismegistus and Plato.

Poetry, the theme of the next 24 lines, is one that comes close to the plans, ambitions and uncertainties of the young Milton, also revealed in the almost contemporary Sonnet VII, 'How soon hath time', and in *Lycidas*. In *L'Allegro* the passage which corresponds to this one is brief, and seems to refer to the actual stage performance of comedies:

Then to the well-trod stage anon,
If *Jonson's* learned Sock be on,

> Or sweetest *Shakespeare*, fancy's child,
> Warble his native Wood-notes wild.   [*131-4*]

The lines too are devoted to poets whose lives overlapped with
Milton's own. The passage in *Il Penseroso* is very different,
beginning, as it does, with Greek tragedy, and evidently pre-
supposing the experience of a student rather than a spectator. The
plays referred to are tragedies rather than comedies. The lines
which follow are among the most moving in the poem, dealing
as they do with poets whose names have survived although their
works have not, or with those, Chaucer and Spenser, who have
died, leaving great works incomplete. Time is still a central
theme, but time in its unpredictable relationship to the creative
imagination.

62 lines have now been devoted to night; they are followed
by 34, divided into one group of 10 and another of 24, concerned
with day. Morning, the appropriately subdued Aurora, is the
subject of the 10-line group [*121-30*], and it should perhaps be
kept in mind that she was the mother of the black Prince Memnon
and his sister, mentioned in line *18* as possible distant likenesses
of Melancholy herself. The sister's name incidentally was
Hemera,[39] a word which means 'day', but one presumably as
overcast as that now described. The slow passage of time is conveyed by a single vivid detail, the 'minute-drops from off the
Eaves' in line *130*. The 24 lines devoted to the part of the day
illuminated by the sun are full of the numinous quality already
mentioned, culminating in 'th'unseen Genius of the Wood', a
brief reference, which nevertheless calls to mind the Attendant
Spirit as the Guardian of the Wood in *Comus*.

These 24 lines are followed by the 12 [*155-66*], which
evoke, not so much 'the studious Cloister's pale' [*156*], as the
music in chapel:

> Service high and Anthems clear,
> As may with sweetness, through mine ear,
> Dissolve me into ecstasies,
> And bring all Heav'n before mine eyes.   [*163-6*]

Once more 12 is a link between time and eternity.

The final 10 lines [167–76] divide into 8, the hermit's life prayed for as the poet's old age, and 2, the concluding couplet. The 8 should perhaps be regarded as a separate unit, expressing aspirations towards the ogdoadic state mentioned in chapter 3.

The analysis has more or less limited itself to *Il Penseroso*, because it is my belief that *L'Allegro*, apart from its companion piece, has no significant numerological structure, and that Milton intended some of the imaginative effect of the paired poems to come from a recognition of that fact. *Il Penseroso* embodies a much greater imaginative and intellectual impulse than its charming feather-brained sister. Folly is subliminally (and therefore doubly effectively) present in much of the imagery of *L'Allegro*; the lark for pre-romantic Europe was a symbol, not of spiritual freedom, but of foolish stereotyped behaviour; the cock on his dunghill was proverbial.[40] A phrase like 'Then to come *in spite of sorrow*' [line 45; my italics] is unexpected but deliberate; it shows the cheerful man consciously turning away from the sorrow in the world. The genealogy of Melancholy which opens the poem is afterwards proved spurious, but there is no subsequent reply to the charge laid in *Il Penseroso* against 'vain deluding joys' that they are 'the brood of folly without father bred' [1–2]. Above all, in *L'Allegro* Plato makes no appearance, and Platonism, one might say, is the touchstone of Renaissance and post-Renaissance numerology.

Appendix. Other Traditions

The poems and prose works discussed in chapters three, four and five belong to a learned Christian-Platonic tradition which scarcely survived the seventeenth century and the combined assault of the new astronomy and the secular philosophies of the Enlightenment. The latest exponent known to me is the Scottish Gaelic poet Alasdair Mac Mhaighstir Alasdair (Alexander MacDonald, c.1690–c.1770), whose 'Song to Winter', *Oran a' Gheamhraidh,* first published in 1751, I have discussed elsewhere.[1] Here the astronomy is so consciously archaic that it must reflect a decision to make use of a science appropriate to the golden age which provided the poet with his metaphors. The contrast with James Thomson (1700–48), whose poetry in other respects provided a model for Mac Mhaighstir Alasdair, is marked. Thomson was a Newtonian, who constantly revised his masterpiece, *The Seasons,* with the result that in almost every edition the number of lines varied, substantially,[2] but not, at least for the numerological critic, significantly. The Christian-Platonic tradition had contributed to the development of Newtonian science, and Thomson retained not a few of its characteristic features—the concept, for instance, of the Great Chain of Being, which finds as vivid expression in him as in Macrobius. The distinctive elements in the Newtonian synthesis, however, were irreconcilable with traditional numerological form.

It is necessary at this point to move backwards, or at least sideways. Numerology is not necessarily Christian or Platonic; theoretically there is no limit to the number of alternative systems possible. Any culture or any religion may have its own series of beliefs associated with numbers, which may, in turn, be expressed in some kind of literary form. During the past two thousand years only a minority even of Christians have been Platonists, and many Christians have not been well instructed in the doctrines and documents of their faith, simply because they were not literate. Yet prose and poetry, orally composed and transmitted by non-literate singers and story-tellers, shows clear traces of numerological structure.

In the longer version of the ballad *Clerk Saunders*,[3] preserved in the first volume of David Herd's MS (British Library, Additional MS 22311), will be found the following seven stanzas:

In and came her seven brothers,
    And all their torches burning bright;
Says thay, We hae but ae sister,
    And see there her lying wi a knight.

Out and speaks the first of them,
    'A wat they hay been lovers dear;'
Out and speaks the next of them,
    'They hae been in love this many a year.'

Out an speaks the third of them,
    'It wear great sin this twa to twain;'
Out an speaks the fourth of them,
    'It wear a sin to kill a sleeping man.'

Out an speaks the fifth of them,
    'A wat they'll near be twaind by me;'
Out an speaks the sixt of them,
    'We'l tak our leave an gae our way.'

Out an speaks the seventh of them,
    'Altho there wear no a man but me,

. . . .

    I bear the brand, I'le gar him die.'

Out he has taen a bright long brand,
    And he has striped it throw the straw,
And throw and throw Clarke Sanders' body
    A wat he has gard cold iron gae.

Sanders he started, an Margret she lapt,
    Intill his arms whare she lay,

> And well and wellsom was the night,
> A wat it was between these twa.   [10-16]

The oral-formulaic nature of these stanzas is self-evident. In much popular belief, 7 is 'chancy', a magic or ill-omened number, and this belief governs both the number of brothers assigned to Marg'ret, and the number of stanzas in which the killing of Saunders by one is dramatised. If the second part of the ballad is accepted as part of the original, the return by night of Saunders to Marg'ret's window, and the account he gives of life in the after-world, are the almost inevitable consequences of the murder in which 7 played so prominent a part.

A more elaborate oral example, also involving the number 7, is to be found in *Manawydan son of Llyr*,[4] the third of the four branches of the Welsh *Mabinogi*, now generally believed to have been first reduced from oral transmission to writing in the second half of the eleventh century. The story is a variant of the international popular tale known as *Placidas (Eustacius)* (AT 938), and in Eastern versions as *The Offended Deity* (AT 939),[5] the central situation being that a prince offends a supernatural power, and as a consequence loses wife, family and worldly goods. His patient behaviour in the face of adversity eventually leads to the restoration of all three. *Job* and *Pericles Prince of Tyre*, Shakespeare's version of the earlier *Apollonius of Tyre*, are literary developments of the same tale. In the Welsh version, the supernatural being, Llwyd son of Cil Coed, is offended by the cruel game of Badger in the Bag, which in *Pwyll Prince of Dyfed*, the first branch of the *Mabinogi*, forced Gwawl son of Clud to give up his claim to the hand in marriage of Rhiannon daughter of Hefeydd the Old. Instead she married Pwyll, prince of the seven cantrefs of Dyfed in south-west Wales, by whom she became the mother of Pryderi. After the death of Pwyll, Rhiannon married Manawydan son of Llyr, who as a consequence also became prince of Dyfed. Unfortunately he inherited the quarrel which began with the game of Badger in the Bag. The third branch of the *Mabinogi* begins with the marriage of Manawydan and Rhiannon, after which the enchanter's revenge begins.

There are 7 stages which occupy seven years:

1. The flocks and herds, which give Manawydan, Rhiannon, Pryderi and Cigfa (Pryderi's wife) their livelihood, disappear, together with the companions who formed their court.

2. Manawydan and Pryderi attempt to make a living as saddlemakers, but are so successful that rival saddlemakers prepare to kill them. Manawydan abandons the craft.

3. The same happens when they become shieldmakers,

4. and when they become shoemakers.

5. They return to Dyfed and live by hunting. The hunting dogs, together with Pryderi and Rhiannon, are magically spirited away.

6. Manawydan once more tries shoemaking—with the same result as before.

7. He returns once more to Dyfed and becomes a peasant farmer, cultivating wheat on 3 crofts, on two of which the mature crop is destroyed on the night before harvest. On the 3rd night he watches the 3rd croft and sees the crop destroyed by a host of mice. He captures one, which is pregnant. Despite Cigfa's objections, he decides to hang it on the Gorsedd, the fairy mound beside the hall in which he and Cigfa live. He erects a gallows.

No stranger had been in Dyfed for seven years. Three separate travellers now appear and attempt to ransom the mouse:

(i) A Clerk offers 1 pound.

(ii) A Priest offers 3 pounds.

(iii) A Bishop makes 3 attempts, offering: (a) 7 pounds; (b) 24 pounds [$3 \times 7 + 3$]; (c) His riding horses, together with 7 loads of baggage on seven sumpter horses. Manawydan refuses all 3, and instead imposes 7 prudent conditions on the bishop, who proves to be the enchanter:

(i) that Rhiannon and Pryderi be set free; (ii) that the charm and the enchantment be removed from the seven cantrefs of Dyfed; (iii) that the identity of the pregnant mouse be revealed (she is the enchanter's wife); (iv) that her motive (to avenge Gwawl son of Clud) for harrying the fields be revealed; (v) that there never henceforth be any spell upon the 7 cantrefs of Dyfed; (vi) that vengeance never be taken upon Pryderi and

Rhiannon, nor upon Manawydan; (vii) that Manawydan should see Pryderi and Rhiannon with him free.

When all seven have been fulfilled, Manawydan releases the mouse, who is changed into a beautiful young woman when her husband strikes her with a magic wand.

When opportunity finally offers, Manawydan is prepared to strike back at the enchanter, but obviously it only arises as a result of his previous exemplary patience.

The story is clearly constructed on numerological principles involving the numbers 7 and 3. Equally clearly, neither number has any Platonic or biblical significance. They are used because they were regarded as numbers peculiarly appropriate for magical beliefs and practices, especially in this case these associated with kingship. The telling of the story was a ritual way of ensuring that Dyfed was never again subjected to the devastation from which it had been rescued by the prudent behaviour of Manawydan. The abstract numerical structure facilitated the recollection in detail of the stages involved in the devastation and eventual recovery.

Mnemonic and magical numerology of this kind is common in oral and folk literature. *Clerk Saunders* provides another example. But it is not confined to oral and folk literature—even in Plato himself, there is no need to deny the presence of something which nowadays we should call magic. During the Renaissance, as has been shown, numerology was exploited, not only by the literary man, but also by the professional *magus,* who believed that knowledge and control of numbers led to power over things, persons and spirits, a belief with deep and ancient roots in the human spirit. It is very likely that Henryson and Spenser convinced themselves that the elaborate representational structure of their poems conferred on poet and enlightened reader a measure at least of power over the object represented—that these poems, in other words, were in some sense instruments of magic.

Even in terms of literature, the process may go back very far. At the beginning of chapter three I commented on the comparative lack of numerological structures in classical literary compositions. Primarily I was then referring to post-Platonic times, and to works which encapsulate in their form a Platonic way of regarding the universe, and in these terms I see no reason to modify my opinion. Earlier Greek literature, however, is characterised by the elaborately structured choral ode, best known from the works of Pindar (c.552–442 BC), Bacchylides (born c.524 BC), and the choruses of tragic drama. It would be the work of many years to show whether or not these structures, often involving strophe, antistrophe and epode, were based on some kind of numerological principle. Here I shall do no more than refer to an earlier, relatively simple, example, the *Partheneion* or Maiden Song, composed by the Spartan poet Alcman, who lived in the second half of the seventh century BC.[6] The *Partheneion,* which seems originally to have consisted of ten 14-line stanzas, was ritually performed before dawn at the festival of the goddess Ortheia, patroness of agriculture, wild animals, fertility, birth and the moon. The choir consisted of 10 girls, among whom two, Hagesichora and Agido, were leaders. Agido's function was to summon the sun to shine, at a time when the moon was still above the horizon—not improbably, that is to say, at the end of the night of full moon, when the moon would set as the sun rose.

The poem is fragmentary and the total evidence small, but at least it does not seem impossible that the 10 stanzas should correspond to the 10 girls who formed the choir, and that the 14 lines of each stanza should correspond to full moon, which occurs on the 14th night of the lunar month. It seems likely[7] that the poem fell into halves, the first 5 stanzas telling the myth of the sons of Hippocoon, slain by Herakles for offences which involved the interests of the goddess, while the second 5, which alone have survived, were devoted to the members of the choir, in particular the praise of Hagesichora, their leader, and to the contention with the rival choir known as the Peleiades. This latter name may mean either 'Doves' or the cluster of 7 readily visible stars known as the Pleiades. The beauty of the girls, and in particular their leader, and the result of the contest between the choirs, may have had special significance in the ritual of Ortheia; the quality and effectiveness of the poet's verses may well also have contributed to its efficacy.

The importance of numerological structures as mnemonics is the final point I wish to emphasise. In days when books were scarce and valuable objects, memory had a practical importance which nowadays is much diminished. With its help, the learned man carried in his head a much larger proportion of his knowledge than does his modern counterpart. In particular, knowledge which in any sense was secret tended to be preserved with the minimum expenditure of paper. Elaborate Arts of Memory were constructed to aid in the process.[8] Among these, I suggest, were the numerological structures discussed in this book. Once they had been grasped, it was easier to store them in the mind and recall them at will for purposes of quotation, teaching or meditation. The last seems likely to have been the most frequent use, but there is no need to ignore any of the others. Numerology, that is to say, had a practical as well as a representational, aesthetic and magical function.

Notes

Chapter One. *Acrostics, Numbers and the Bible*

1 *De architectura* was edited by F. Krohn in the Teubner series (Lipsiae 1912). The translation used is that of Morris Hicky Morgan, *Vitruvius. The Ten Books on Architecture* (Cambridge, Mass. 1914; paperback, New York 1960).

 See also and in general, Graham Flegg, *Numbers. Their History and Meaning* (London 1983). The Babylonian numeral system, which has left many traces in modern systems of mensuration, took advantage of the properties of 6 by using 60 as a base. The advantages of a duodecimal as opposed to a decimal system, derive largely from the same source.

2 See especially Arthur O. Lovejoy, *The Great Chain of Being* (Cambridge, Mass. 1936), cap. VI, 'The Chain of Being in Eighteenth-Century Thought', and 'Man's Place and Role in Nature', E. M. W. Tillyard, *The Elizabethan World Picture* (London 1943), 60-73.

3 Below, 59-60.

4 Howard Candler, 'On the Symbolic Use of Numbers in the *Divina Commedia* and Elsewhere', *Transactions of the Royal Society of Literature, Second Series*, XXX (1910), 1-29. But even this is later than the recognition of numerological qualities in the *Vita Nuova*. See K. McKenzie, 'The Symmetrical Structure of Dante's *Vita Nuova*', *Publications of the Modern Language Association of America*, XVIII (1903), 341ff. C. E. Norton (1827-1908) 'was the first scholar to make public his observation of this symmetrical pattern' in his *The 'New Life' of Dante Alighieri*, published in 1859, but 'twenty years earlier Gabriele Rossetti (1783-1854) had seen the essential outline of it, as is clear from a letter of his to Charles Lyell dated January 13, 1836'. The quotations are from Charles S. Singleton, *An Essay on the Vita Nuova* (Cambridge, Mass. 1949), 150.

5 C. Butler, *Number Symbolism* (London 1970), 97.

6 *European Literature and the Latin Middle Ages,* translated by Willard R. Trask (London 1953), Appendix 15, 'Numerical Composition', 501-9.

7 Gilbert Murray, *Five Stages of Greek Religion*, edition of 1935, 142.

8   See especially Dame Frances A. Yates, *The Art of Memory* (London 1966), 175-96, and the references there given.

The *ars combinatoria* resulted from a vision experienced by Lull in or about 1272 on Mount Randa in Majorca. In this he saw what he called the Dignities of God—for example, the goodness, greatness, eternity, power, wisdom, will, virtue, truth, glory of his *Ars magna*—infusing creation, or, to put it in a reverse order which corresponds more closely to the experience, saw how creation participated in a Christian version of the Platonic Forms. The vision contained many features which paralleled aspects of the Jewish Cabbala and Moslem Sufism (both important in the Iberian peninsula during Lull's lifetime), but was specially significant because it seemed to offer evidence for the priority of an ultimately trinitarian, and therefore Christian, structure. The various forms of the Art derived from this vision were thus primarily agencies for the conversion to Christianity of Jews and Moslems; some had secondary purposes, but in all the aim was to produce mathematically constructed combinations (hence *ars combinatoria*) of the Dignities among themselves and in relation to the created world. 'The Divine Dignities form into triadic structures, reflected from them down through the whole creation; as causes they inform the whole creation through its elemental structure. An Art based on them constructs a method by which ascent can be made on the ladder of creation to the Trinity at its apex' (Yates, *op. cit.*, 180).

9   1.8; 22.13.

10 J. Hastings (ed.), *Dictionary of the Bible* (7th impression, Edinburgh 1929), s.v. 'Number'.

11 G. Keynes (ed.), *The Works of Sir Thomas Browne* (4 vols, London, 1964), 1.222-3, more readily available in Keynes (ed.), *Sir Thomas Browne Selected Writings* (London 1968, paperback 1970), 206-7. See also the notes in L. C. Martin (ed.), *Sir Thomas Browne, Religio Medici and Other Works* (Oxford 1964), 369.

12 That is, in the Mosaic Law, revealed long after the death of Abraham to his descendant, Moses. The Law existed from eternity, although it was revealed at a specific time.

13 *Binah:* the 3rd of 10 *Sefirot* or Emanations of God. 'The organic symbolism equates the primordial point with the seed sown in the womb of "the supernal mother", who is *Binah*' (*Encyclopaedia Judaica* [Jerusalem 1972], X.574). It is interesting that the sidenote to Browne's text refers the reader to *Cabalistarum selectiora obscurioraque dogmata, a Ioanne Pico ex eorum commentationibus pridem excerpta, et ab Archangelo Burgonavensi Minoritano, nunc primum*

luculentissimis interpretationibus illustrata. This book, written by Archangelo de Burgo Nuova, and published at Venice in 1569, is an exposition of the 72 Cabalist *Conclusiones* of Pico della Mirandola, to be found on pp.107‑111 of the 1572 edition of his works. The importance of Pico for Renaissance numerology is indicated in chapter 5 below. Pico's conclusions are 72 in number because the mystic Name of God is formed by the names of 72 angels. See Johannes Reuchlin (1455‑1522), *De Arte Cabalistica* (Haguenau 1517).

The information in this note is largely derived from Frances A. Yates, *Giordano Bruno and the Hermetic Tradition* (London 1964, paperback 1978), chapter v, 'Pico della Mirandola and Cabalist Magic'. In general, I am much indebted to Dame Frances' work.

14 G. B. Caird, *The Revelation of St John the Divine* (London 1966), 174‑6.

15 H. St J. Thackeray, *Josephus* (8 vols, Loeb Classical Library, London and New York 1926‑65), 1.178‑81.

16 *Biblia Sacra Vulgatae Editionis* (Nova Editio, Paris 1868), v. The adjective *galeatus,* applied to a prologue or preface, means 'in which one defends oneself'.

17 J. H. Bernard and R. Atkinson, *The Irish Liber Hymnorum* (2 vols, Henry Bradshaw Society, XIII, XIV, London 1898), 2.25‑6.

18 *Reflections on the Psalms* (London 1958; paperback ed., 1961), 52‑3. Lewis comments that the acrostic form 'may have given an ancient or something of the same sort of pleasure we get from the Italian metre called the *Sestina,* where instead of rhymes we have the same end words repeated in varying orders in each stanza'. This seems to me rather inadequate.

19 Above, footnote 9.

20 2 vols, Oxford 1896.

21 1.lix, footnote 8.

22 Carl Selmer, *Navigatio Sancti Brendani Abbatis* (Notre Dame 1959).

23 James F. Kenney, *The Sources for the Early History of Ireland: Ecclesiastical* (New York 1929), 415.

24 2 vols, Oxford 1910. The verses are printed, 11.293‑4.

25 *Exodus* 3.2ff.

26 F. J. E. Raby, *A History of Christian‑Latin Poetry from the Beginning to the Close of the Middle Ages* (2nd edit., Oxford 1953), 369.

27 *Revelation* 12, 3‑4.

28 *Revelation* 13, 7‑8.

29 *Matthew* 4, 19.

30 The best known is the Anglo-Norman verse *Voyage of St Brendan*. See especially E. G. R. Waters, *The Anglo-Norman Voyage of St Brendan by Benedeit* (Oxford 1928): M. Dominica Legge, *Anglo-Norman Literature and its Background* (Oxford 1963), 8-18.

31 Plummer, *Vitae Sanctorum Hiberniae,* i.xxxvi-xliii.

Chapter Two. *Plato. The Harmonic Soul of the Universe*

1 Paul Shorey (ed. and trans.), *Plato* vi. *Republic* ii (Cambridge, Mass. and London, Loeb Classical Library 1935), 499-505 (*Republic* x, 616b-617d).

2 Frances A. Yates, *Giordano Bruno and the Hermetic Tradition* (London 1964: paperback ed., 1978), 152.

3 The quotation is from J. Adam (ed.), *The Republic of Plato* (2 vols, Cambridge 1902), ii.473-4. Craigie's note will be found in B. Jowett and L. Campbell, *Plato's Republic* (3 vols, Oxford 1894), iii 475-6; Cook Wilson's in *Classical Review,* xvi (1902), 292-3.

4 H. D. P. Lee (trans.), *Plato. Timaeus and Critias* (Harmondsworth 1971), 46-8 (*Timaeus,* 34b-36d).

5 Lee, *op. cit.,* 47.

6 J. H. Waszink (ed.), *Timaeus a Calcidio Translatus Commentarioque Instructus* (*Corpus Platonicum Medii Aevi,* London and Leyden 1962), 89-92.

7 W. H. Stahl (trans.), *Macrobius. Commentary on the Dream of Scipio* (New York and London 1952), 192-3. The text of the *Commentary* forms the second volume of J. Willis (ed.) *Macrobii Opera* (2 vols, Leipzig 1963).

8 See below, chapter 5.

9 Lee, *op. cit.,* 47-8.

10 Above, footnote 6.

11 Lee, *op. cit.,* 48.

12 Waszink, *op. cit.,* 98-9.

13 Lee, *op. cit.,* 57-8.

14 J. N. Findlay, *Plato. The Written and Unwritten Doctrines* (London and New York 1974), xi.

15 *Op. cit.,* 247 (*Republic* viii.546b-d).

16 *Op. cit.,* 197-8. The reference is to Adam, *op. cit.,* ii.264-312. See also Alastair Fowler, *Spenser and the Numbers of Time* (London 1964), 36-44.

17 Edith Hamilton and Huntington Cairns (eds.), *The Collected Dialogues of Plato* (Princeton 1973), 1323, 1325, 1329, 1330-1 (*Laws,* translated by A. E. Taylor, 737e-738a: 740b-d: 745b-e: 746d-747a). The 59 factors are 1, 2, 3, 4, 5, 6, 7, 8, 9, 10, 12, 14,

15, 16, 18, 20, 21, 24, 28, 30, 35, 36, 40, 42, 45, 48, 56, 60, 63, 70, 72, 80, 84, 90, 105, 112, 120, 126, 140, 144, 168, 180, 210, 240, 252, 280, 315, 336, 360, 420, 504, 560, 630, 720, 840, 1008, 1260, 1680, 2520.

18 Hamilton and Cairns, *op. cit.,* 1520 (*Epinomis,* translated by A. E. Taylor, 977a-b).

19 C. W. Keyes (ed. and trans.), *Cicero* XVI. *De Re Publica. De Legibus* (Cambridge, Mass. and London, Loeb Classical Library 1928).

20 Above, footnote 7.

21 Stahl, *op. cit.,* 71.

22 Stahl, *op. cit.,* 73.

23 Stahl, *op. cit.,* 73-4.

24 Stahl, *op. cit.,* 188-9.

25 Stahl, *op. cit.,* 99-100.

26 Boethius, *The Consolations of Music, Logic, Theology, and Philosophy* (Oxford 1981), 72.

27 *Op. cit.,* 73. See also, John Caldwell, 'The *De Institutione Arith-metica* and the *De Institutione Musica*'; David Pingree, 'Boethius' Geometry and Astronomy'; Alison White, 'Boethius in the Medieval Quadrivium'; all in Margaret Gibson (ed.), *Boethius, His Life, Thought and Influence* (Oxford 1981), 135-205.

28 *Op. cit.,* 81.

Chapter Three. *Node of Intersection. Celts and Carolingians*

1 See especially G. Duckworth, *Structural Patterns and Proportions in the Aeneid* (Ann Arbor, 1962); Curtius, *op. cit.,* 502-3.

2 Text in George E. McCracken and others (eds. and trs.), *Saint Augustine The City of God against the Pagans* (7 vols., London and Cambridge, Mass., Loeb Classical Library, 1954-). The translation used is that by H. Bettenson in D. Knowles (ed.), *Augustine City of God* (Pelican Books 1972).

3 Knowles, *op. cit.,* 311 (VIII,9).

4 *The Evolution of Medieval Thought* (London 1962), 49.

5 *Evolution of Medieval Thought,* 55-8.

6 Translated by J. Parker (2 vols, London, 1897-9). Greek text in Migne, *Patrologia Graeca,* 3 and 4. In view of the significance later attached to the number 15, it is noteworthy that the main source of symbolical angel lore for the later middle ages was the 15th chapter of the *Celestial Hierarchy*

7 Migne, *Patrologia Latina,* 122.1023-94. 'Shortly before 860 he was asked by Charles the Bald to make a new translation of the writings attributed to Dionysius the Areopagite, of which a copy had been presented to Charles's father, Louis the Debonair, by

the Emperor Michael the Stammerer in 827' (I. P. Sheldon-Williams, *Iohannis Scotti Erivgenae Periphyseon* [*De Divisione Naturae*] *Liber Primus,* Dublin 1978), 3.

8 F. J. E. Raby (ed.), *Oxford Book of Medieval Latin Verse* (Oxford 1959). *Apparebit repentina* is no. 13 of the collection (pp.14-15), *A solis ortus* no. 30 (pp.39-42).

9 Willis, *op. cit.* The *Saturnalia* occupies the first volume.

10 Curtius, *op. cit.,* 445 (Appendix V, 'Late Antique Literary Studies').

11 Stahl, *op. cit.,* 108.

12 I. P. Sheldon-Williams, with the collaboration of Ludwig Bieler (eds), *Iohannis Scotti Erivgenae Periphyseon* (Dublin, 1968-).

13 Bernard and Atkinson, *op. cit.,* 1.66-81, but most readily consulted in Raby, *op. cit.,* 59-68.

14 Above, Chap. I, 11.

15 Stahl, *op. cit.,* 104.

16 'But the Quincunx of Heaven runs low, and 'tis time to close the five ports of knowledge.' Sir Thomas Browne, *The Garden of Cyrus* (Keynes, *op. cit.,* 210).

17 Stahl, *op. cit.,* 98-9.

18 Stahl, *op. cit.,* 97.

19 For example, *Hymnus Sancti Secundini, Lamentatio Sancti Ambrosii, Hymnus Lasriani,* Bernard and Atkinson, *op. cit.,* 1.7-13, 137-42, 158.

20 F. E. Warren (ed.) (Henry Bradshaw Society, IV, X, 2 vols, 1893-5).

21 Warren, *op. cit.,* II.44. Raby, *op. cit.,* 70-1.

22 Warren, *op. cit.,* II.28. Raby, *op. cit.,* 69-70.

23 L. Traube (ed.), *Monumenta Germaniae Historica: Poetae Latini Aevi Carolini,* III (Berlin 1896), 427-517.

24 *Op. cit.,* 506.

25 Lee, *op. cit.,* 41, 42, 51 (*Timaeus* 29a-b, 30d, 37e).

26 Stahl, *op. cit.,* 104-5.

27 Stahl, *op. cit.,* 94-9.

28 Stahl, *op. cit.,* 99-117.

29 Murray, *op. cit.,* 147-8, 'Above the Moon there is no Chance, only Necessity; there is the will of the other six Kosmokratores, Rulers of the Universe. But above them all there is an Eighth region—they call it simply the Ogdoas—the home of the Ultimate God'. In the early Christian-Gnostic heresy of Valentinus (2nd century) 'founded on the Platonic conception of a parallelism between the world of ideas ($\pi\lambda\acute{\eta}\rho\omega\mu\alpha$) and the world of phenomena ($\kappa\acute{\epsilon}\nu\omega\mu\alpha$)' [*ODCC,* s.v. 'Valentinus'], the $\pi\lambda\acute{\eta}\rho\omega\mu\alpha$ is primarily the abode of eight Aeons, the Ogdoad, to which the

lesser Decad and Dodecad are immediately subordinate. 'At the head of all things invisible and ineffable is the Supreme Being, the Father, the un-begotten Abyss, with his consort Sigé (Silence). When it pleased the father to produce other beings, he impregnates Sigé, who presents him with a being like himself, the Intellect (Νοῦς), and also a female, who is to the Intellect what Sigé is to the Abyss. The consort of the Intellect is the Truth. The Abyss and Sigé, the Intellect and the Truth, form the first four Aeons, the first Tetrad. From Intellect and Truth were born the Word and the Life; and from these again Man and the Church. Thus was completed the Ogdoad, the company of eight higher Aeons' (L. Duchesne, *Early History of the Christian Church* [3 vols, London, 1909-24], I.120). According to this system, the Demiurge, who created the material universe, is the creation of Hachamoth, herself the illegitimate offspring of Wisdom (Σοφία), the female Aeon who occupies the lowest position in the Dodecad. Hachamoth was expelled from the πλήρωμα; it was her creature who formed the κένωμα, which he governs together with the other planetary powers. Together they form the Hebdomad. Salvation for some prisoners of the material creation is eventually assured by the production of the significantly numbered 33rd Aeon (a sixteenth pair, Christ and the Holy Spirit, had already been produced), who is Jesus the Saviour.

Such systems were not necessarily heretical. In the apocryphal but orthodox *Testament of Our Lord in Galilee*, written in Greek c.150, but preserved only in Ethiopic, Coptic, and a single Latin leaf, the risen Christ declares, 'I have come into the Ogdoad, which is the Lord's day'. The Resurrection on the eighth day is here identified with the ogdoadic state. The hymn sung by Jesus and his disciples before his trial and Crucifixion, preserved in the apocryphal (and probably Docetic) *Acts of John* (not later than the early third century) contains the words, 'The Ogdoad singeth praise with us. The number Twelve danceth on high. The Whole on high hath part in our dancing'. (Both examples are taken from M. R. James [ed. and trs.], *Apocryphal New Testament* [Oxford 1924], the first from p.491, the second from p.253.)

30 247c-248c (Hamilton and Cairns, *op. cit.*, 494-5).
31 Stahl, *op. cit.*, 133-7.
32 Paul von Winterfeld (ed.), *Monumenta Germaniae Historica: Poetae Latini Aevi Carolini*, IV.i (Berlin 1899), 265-71.
33 Curtius, *op. cit.*, 508-9.
34 Traube, *op. cit.*, 562-5.
35 M. Gerbert, *Scriptores ecclesiastici de musica sacra potissimum* (3 vols, St Blasien 1784).

36 Denis Stevens, 'The Birth of Organized Polyphony', in Denis
Stevens and Alec Robertson, *Pelican History of Music*
(Harmondsworth 1960), I.212.

37 Gerbert, *op. cit.* See the article 'Musica enchiriadis' in
S. Sadie (ed.), *New Grove Dictionary of Music and Musicians*
(London 1980).

38 *Neue Wege zur dichterischen und musikalischen Technik Walthers
von der Vogelweide* (Utrecht 1950).

39 'Secular Monody', Stevens and Robertson, *op. cit.,* 256⁄7.

40 'Ars Nova', Stevens and Robertson, *op. cit.,* 274.

41 Numerological composition remains important in music almost
to the present day. See, for instance, Friedrich Smend, *Johann
Sebastian Bach bei seinem Namen gerufen* (Kassel 1950) and Lionel
Pike, *Beethoven, Sibelius and the Profound Logic* (London 1978).

Chapter Four. *The Transition to the Vernaculars*

1 Carl J. Odenkirchen (ed. and trs.), *The Life of St Alexius*
(Brookline, Mass. and Leyden 1978). See also E. W. Bulatkin,
'The Arithmetical Structure of the O.F. *Vie de Saint Alexis*',
PMLA LXXIV (1959), 495⁄502. Bulatkin's paper partly derives
from A. Granville Hatcher, 'The Old French Poem *St Alexis*:
A Mathematical Demonstration', *Traditio* 8 (1952), 111⁄58, and
H. Lausberg, 'Zum *Alexiuslied*', *Archiv für das Studium der neueren
Sprachen* 191 (1955), 202⁄13, and 195 (1958), 141⁄4.

It seems probable that in older forms of the legend Rome meant,
not the Italian metropolis, but New Rome, Constantinople.

Studies of early vernacular works—for instance, Thomas
Elwood Hart, 'Tectonic Methodology and an application to
Beowulf', Edward G. Fichtner, 'Patterns of Arithmetical Pro⁄
portion in the *Nibelungenlied*' (Caroline D. Eckhardt (ed.),
Essays in the Numerical Criticism of Medieval Literature, Lewisburg
and London, 1980, 185⁄230)—although related to the present
study, are not, and probably would not claim to be, numerological,
as the term has been used in this book.

2 Sir Paul Harvey and J. E. Heseltine, *The Oxford Companion to
French Literature* (Oxford 1959), *s.v. Alexis, Vie de Saint.*

3 P. Stone (trs.), *Sir Gawain and the Green Knight* (Harmondsworth
1959), 49⁄50. The standard text is N. Davis's revision of the
edition by J. R. R. Tolkien and E. V. Gordon (Oxford 1967),
where the passage quoted occupies lines 625⁄65.

With the reference to Solomon, compare the account of the
Ship of Solomon in the *Queste del Saint Graal,* mentioned above,
p. 78.

4 Albert Pauphilet (ed.), *La Queste del Saint Graal* (Paris 1923):

P. M. Matarasso (trs.), *The Quest of the Holy Grail* (Harmonds-worth 1969).

5 See Jean Frappier, 'The Vulgate Cycle' in R. S. Loomis (ed.), *Arthurian Literature in the Middle Ages* (Oxford 1959), 295-318. The Prose *Lancelot* occupies vols III-VI of H. O. Sommer (ed.), *Livre d'Artus* (7 vols, Paris 1908-13).

6 Matarasso, *op. cit.*, 133.

7 Matarasso, *op. cit.*, 207-21.

8 The idea goes back at least as far as St Augustine's commentary on the Psalms: *numerus ternarius ad animum pertinet, quaternarius ad corpus* (Migne, *PL*, XXXVI-XXXVII, col. 91), but was much elaborated in such later authors as Hugh of St Victor (*PL*, CLXXV, col. 400 *et seq.*).

9 Émile Mâle, *The Gothic Image. Religious Art in France of the Thirteenth Century*, trs. Dora Nussey (Paris 1910; English translation, London 1913; paperback, London and Glasgow 1961), 14.

10 Stahl, *op. cit.*, 98.

11 T. Okey and P. H. Wicksteed (eds and trs.), *The Vita Nuova and Canzoniere of Dante Alighieri* (London 1906). Because it first introduced me to Dante, and I still admire the precision and felicity, in particular of the verse renderings, I have usually quoted the translation which D. G. Rossetti included in *The Early Italian Poets* (London 1861), reprinted in the Everyman *Poems and Translations. Dante Gabriel Rossetti* (London 1912). Here and there I have ventured a small emendation.

12 Charles S. Singleton, *An Essay on the Vita Nuova* (Cambridge, Mass. 1949), 78-9, and the references quoted in cap. 1, footnote 1.

13 Stahl, *op. cit.*, 71.

14 Singleton, *loc. cit.*

15 'The nature of God is a circle of which the centre is everywhere and the circumference is nowhere.' Attributed to Empedocles (fl. c.444 BC).

16 *Conceitful Thought. The Interpretation of English Renaissance Poems* (Edinburgh 1975), 35. The poem referred to is Surrey's 'Epitaph on Clere' (Emrys Jones, *Henry Howard Earl of Surrey Poems*, Oxford 1964, 32).

17 See cap. 3, footnote 6.

18 2 vols, London 1854-6.

19 *Summa Theologica*, 54.5. Anton C. Pegis (ed.), *Basic Writings of Saint Thomas Aquinas* (2 vols, New York 1945), 1.515.

20 Okey and Wicksteed, *op. cit*, 304-9.

21 Okey and Wicksteed, *op. cit*, 125-7.

22 Denton Fox (ed.), *The Poems of Robert Henryson* (Oxford

1981), 65. 'bakkis' from *bak*; 'bat'; 'man's soul is like a bat's eye'.

23   *Op. cit.*, 13.

24   D. S. Brewer (ed.), *The Parlement of Foulys* (London and Edinburgh 1960).

25   Cf. especially the many references to New Year in *Sir Gawain and the Green Knight*. Stanza 3, for instance, begins 'Þis kyng lay at Camylot vpon Krystmasse' (37); the immediately succeeding stanza, 'Wyle Nw Ȝer watz so Ȝep þat hit watz nwe cummen' (60. Davis, Tolkien and Gordon, *op. cit.*, 2). The editors comment (74), 'Though in the Middle Ages the legal and ecclesiastical year began on various dates (in England from the late twelfth century on 25 March, the Annunciation, which continued until 1752), the Roman use of 1 January seems never to have fallen out of popular memory and observance, and the term "New Year's Day" never meant anything else'.

26   E. V. Gordon (ed.), *Pearl* (Oxford 1953). *Sir Gawain and the Green Knight*, it should be noted, also contains 101 stanzas, perhaps indicating that the poet regarded the Arthurian as equivalent to an Otherworldly setting. Cf. the opening of *The Wife of Bath's Tale* (F. N. Robinson, ed., *The Works of Geoffrey Chaucer*, 2nd edition, Boston 1957, 84):

In th'olde dayes of the Kyng Arthour,
Of which that Britons speken greet honour,
Al was this land fulfild of fayerye.
The elf-queene, with hir joly compaignye,
Daunced ful ofte in many a grene mede.
This was the olde opinion, as I rede;
I speke of manye hundred yeres ago.
But now kan no man se none elves mo.   [857-64]

It may be important that the description of the pentangle and its significance is completed in stanza 28 of the entire poem. 28, as has often been noted, is the second perfect number. Stanza 33 describes the miraculous appearance of Bercilak's castle in answer to Gawain's prayer in stanza 32, which ends 'Cros Kryst me spede!'.

For the numerological analysis of *Pearl* and *Sir Gawain and the Green Knight*, see especially A. Kent Hieatt, 'Sir Gawain: pent-angle, *luf-lace*, numerical structure', in A. Fowler (ed.), *Silent Poetry* (London 1970), 116-40, and 'Numerical Structures in Verse: Second-Generation Studies Needed (Exemplified in *Sir Gawain* and the *Chanson de Roland*)', in Caroline D. Eckhardt, *op. cit.*, 65-78.

27   Matthew McDiarmid (ed.), *The Kingis Quair of James Stewart*

(London 1973). See also my own 'The literature of fifteenth-
century Scotland', in Jennifer M. Brown (ed.), *Scottish Society in
the Fifteenth Century* (London 1977), 187-92. In the not-too-
distant future I hope to write at greater length on *The Kingis Quair*.

Chapter Five. *The Renaissance and its Aftermath*

1   On Plethon, see F. Masai, *Pléthon et le Platonisme de Mistra* (Paris
1956). Brief accounts, which differ strikingly in emphasis, are
to be found in Edgar Wind, *Pagan Mysteries in the Renaissance*
(London 1958: enlarged and revised, Harmondsworth 1967),
244-8, and in Steven Runciman, *The Last Byzantine Renaissance*
(Cambridge 1970), 77-80.

In pursuit of the Neoplatonic polytheism, the ritual of which
forms a major surviving part of his *Laws,* itself developed from the
system set out in Plato's *Laws,* Plethon produced 'twenty-seven
hymns of nine verses each . . . based on Platonic numerology
(*Timaeus* 35c)' (Wind, *op. cit.,* 256, referring to C. Alexandre,
ed., *Pléthon, Traité des Lois,* Paris 1858, Book III.xxxv). In
Pléthon's system, Zeus corresponds to the Neoplatonic One,
Poseidon to Mind, Kronos with Helios to the Soul of the World.
The Neoplatonic trinity is thus constituted. Poseidon, eldest
legitimate child of Zeus, aided by his legitimate brothers and
sisters, of whom seven are specified in the *Hymns,* although others
are listed in the *Allocutions,* which in the text precede them, produces whatever is created and eternal. The named seven are, Hera
(Poseidon's sister-wife), Apollo, Artemis, Athena, Dionysus,
Hephaestus, and Pluto. Kronos, eldest illegitimate child of Zeus,
aided by his illegitimate brothers and sisters, the Titans—
Aphrodite (his sister-wife), Pan, Demeter, Kore (Persephone)
are listed—and by Helios (the Sun) and the other planetary gods,
produces whatever is created and mortal. Two groups thus exist,
the Olympian and the Tartarean, linked by paternity and the
marriage of Kore and Pluto. The Olympian divinities correspond
to the Platonic Ideas, and Plethon, one must presume, identified
Poseidon, Mind, with the Idea of the Good.

In addition to the Olympian and Tartarean divinities, there are
also benevolent Daemons, intermediaries between gods and
mortals.

The *Hymns* are addressed to Zeus (4), the Gods generally (3),
Poseidon, Hera, the Olympians as a group (?), Apollo, Artemis,
the Planets, Athena, Dionysus, the Tartareans as a group,
Hephaestus, the Daemons, the Lesser Gods as a group (Tartarean,
Stellar, Planetary and Daemonic), and Pluto, together with 6
'ephemeral' (i.e. daily) hymns, setting out the beliefs, intentions

and aspirations of the worshipper. Each contains 9 lines because $9 = 3 \times 3$, and the total number is 27 because $27 = 3 \times 3 \times 3$, and also because 27 is the final number, the first masculine cube, in the usual formulation of the Lambda series. 3 is the trinity, and as a prime number has 1 (or the One) as its sole factor.

This numerology finds its closest parallel—which remains nevertheless at a considerable distance—in the numerology of Henryson's *New Orpheus,* discussed above.

2   *A Companion to Classical Texts* (Oxford 1913), 100.

3   Petrarch's Greek master was the irascible mathematician, Barlaam of Calabria, who in 1330 had come off second best in a debate with Nicephoras Gregoras, and in 1340 initiated the Hesychast controversy, in which once more he was on the losing side. Barlaam was eventually converted from Orthodox to Catholic Christianity. See especially K. Setton, 'The Byzantine background to the Italian Renaissance', *Proceedings of the American Philosophical Society* 100 (1956).

4   See especially Paul Oskar Kristeller, *The Philosophy of Marsilio Ficino,* trs. by Virginia Conant (New York 1943: reprint Gloucester, Mass. 1964).

5   Ernst Cassirer, Paul Oskar Kristeller, John Herman Randall Jr., *The Renaissance Philosophy of Man* (Chicago and London 1948), 223-54. The translation is by Elizabeth Livermore Forbes.

6   *The Wars of Truth* (Cambridge, Mass. 1952), 309-10.

7   *The Enchanted Glass* (Oxford 1960), 21-2.

8   Craig, *loc. cit.,* where the reference given is Augustine, *De Civitate Dei,* VIII.viii, xvii *et passim.* I have been unable to trace an exact source for the quotation.

9   Craig, *op. cit.,* 17-18. The quotation is from *De occulta Philosophia,* 2.50.

10 Fox, *op. cit.,* 132-53. To clarify the arithmetical and musical terms, I have constructed my own text. See my 'Neoplatonism and Orphism in Fifteenth-Century Scotland. The Evidence of Henryson's *New Orpheus*', *Scottish Studies* 20 (1976), 69-89. On text and title, see especially footnotes 1 and 2.

11 As was first pointed out by David Laing (*The Poems and Fables of Robert Henryson,* Edinburgh 1865, xii). Dr John Durkan first suggested 1468 as the date at which Henryson left Glasgow for Dunfermline (D. Roberts, ed., *Essays on the Scottish Reformation,* Glasgow 1962, 157).

12 For the reading 'Plato', see Laing, *op. cit.,* 57, 251, and my *Robert Henryson* (Oxford 1967), 40, footnote 1. The reading was subsequently adopted by Fox for his edition.

13 In lines 427-34, part of the *Moralitas* subjoined to the poem.

14 Stahl, *op. cit.*, 133-4.

15 Wind, *op. cit.*, Appendix 6, 'Gafurius on the Harmony of the Spheres', 265-9 and plate 20. The emended form 'Hyperlydia' in Henryson (*ypolerica* and *yporlerica* in the print and MSS) corresponds to 'Hypermixolydius' in Gafurius. Fox (*op. cit.*, 411) dismisses on good ground the alternative emendation 'Hypolocria', but fails to see the force of 'Hyperlydia', and characteristically concludes that '*ypolerica* is a not very serious nonce-formation'.

16 Enid Welsford, *Spenser Fowre Hymnes Epithalamion* (Oxford 1967), 102-10.

17 Stahl, *op. cit.*, 136.

18 See, however, Einar Bjorvand, 'Spenser's defence of poetry: some structural aspects of the *Fowre Hymnes*', Maren-Sofie Røstvig (ed.), *Fair Forms* (Cambridge 1975), 13-53.

19 *Op. cit.*, 194. Miss Welsford's Appendix 11, 'Number Symbolism in *Epithalamion*' contains some useful observations on Hieatt's book, as do Max A. Wickert, 'Structure and Ceremony in Spenser's *Epithalamion*', *ELH* 35 (1968), 135-57, and Alastair Fowler, *Triumphal Forms: Structural Patterns in Elizabethan Poetry* (Cambridge 1970), 103-7 and 161-73.

20 *Op. cit.*, 67.

21 *Op. cit.*, 80-1.

22 The cantos first appeared in the folio edition of *The Faerie Queene* (London 1609).

23 *Op. cit.*, 504.

24 Fox, *op. cit.*, 64-75. The reference occurs in Stanza 8, line 53.

25 L. E. Kastner, *The Poetical Works of William Drummond of Hawthornden* (2 vols, STS, Edinburgh and London 1913), 2.37-47.

26 See my *Progress and Poetry* (Edinburgh 1982), 23-6.

27 Kastner, *op. cit.*, 339-41. The relation to Spenser is not here noted.

28 All quotations from Milton are from Merritt Y. Hughes (ed.), *John Milton Complete Poems and Major Prose* (New York 1957).

29 MacQueen, *Progress and Poetry*, loc. cit.

30 Qvarnström, *op. cit.*

31 Røstvig (ed.), *Fair Forms*, 54-84.

32 Fowler (ed.), *Silent Poetry*, 170-84.

33 Yates, *Giordano Bruno and the Hermetic Tradition*, 398-403.

34 See, for instance, the illustration in Wind, *op. cit.*, plate 23, where Hermes is touching his fingers to his lips in a gesture commanding silence, and the concluding words of the 13th Hermetic treatise, where Tat is commanded to maintain silence about the doctrines he has just received (A. D. Nock and A. J. Festugière, *Corpus*

Hermeticum, 4 vols, Paris 1946-54, XIII.22, p.209).

35 See vol. 1 of Festugière, *La Révélation d'Hermès Trismégiste*
   (4 vols, Paris 1950-4): Yates, *Giordano Bruno,* 44-61.

36 W. Scott in *Hermetica* (4 vols, Oxford 1924-36), 2.161-2, has
   the following note on *Corpus Hermeticum* V.4. 'The two Bears, as
   depicted on a celestial globe or planisphere, looked like two
   animals walking in the same direction round the Pole; and this,
   no doubt, suggested the notion that they worked like mill-horses,
   and made the whole sphere of the fixed stars revolve, or that one
   of them did so.' He compares Hermetic Fragment VI in the
   anthology of excerpts compiled in the early 5th century AD by
   Stobaeus. This last lays much greater emphasis on the power of
   the two constellations.

37 *Phaedrus* 246a-257b; *Phaedo* 107c-115a.

38 *Etymologiae* VII.31.

39 'Dictys Cretensis', *De Bello Troiano,* VI.x.

40 MacQueen, *Henryson,* 107-10, 165.

Appendix. *Other Traditions*

1 *Progress and Poetry,* 78-82.

2 See, for example, the textual notes in J. Logie Robertson (ed.),
   James Thomson Poetical Works (London 1908).

3 F. J. Child, *The English and Scottish Popular Ballads* (5 vols,
   Boston 1884-98: reprinted, New York 1965), II.159.

4 Ifor Williams (ed.), *Pedeir Keinc y Mabinogi* (Caerdydd 1930),
   49-65.

5 This is not the usual view; see W. J. Gruffydd, *Rhiannon* (Cardiff
   1953) and K. Jackson, *The International Popular Tale and Welsh
   Tradition* (Cardiff 1961). It seems to me that *Manawydan* is an
   example of the international folk tale in precisely the same way
   that *Culhwch and Olwen,* for instance, is an example of AT 513 A,
   Six go through the whole World.

6 D. L. Page (ed.), *Alcman The Partheneion* (Oxford 1951).

7 Page, *op. cit.,* 1.

8 See especially Frances A. Yates, *The Art of Memory* (London
   1966: paperback 1969).

Bibliography

This bibliography aims at providing no more than a reason-able selection of articles and books, written for the most part during the present century and directly concerned with numerological criticism. Alternatively some few contain relevant background material. Further information may be obtained from such standard publications as *The Year's Work in English Studies, The Year's Work in Modern Language Studies, The Year's Work in Scottish Literary and Linguistic Studies* (published by *Scottish Literary Journal*), the *Bulletin Bibliographique de la Société Internationale Arthurienne,* the *MLA Bibliography,* and the *International Medieval Bibliography.*

Austin, H, D. 'Number and Geometrical Design in the *Divine Comedy*', *The Personalist* XVI (1925).

Baker, Herschel. *The Dignity of Man* (Cambridge, Mass., 1947).

—— *The Wars of Truth* (Cambridge, Mass., 1952).

Batts, Michael S. 'Numerical Structure in Medieval Literature', in Stanley N. Werbow (ed.), *Formal Aspects of Medieval German Poetry. A Symposium* (Austin, Texas, 1969).

Baybak, Michael. See under Fowler, Alastair (ed.).

Benini, Rodolfo. *Dante tra gli splendori de' suoi enigmi risolti, ed altri saggi* (Rome, 1952).

Bjorvand, Einar. See under Røstvig, Maren-Sofie (ed.).

Brooks, Douglas. See under Fowler, Alastair (ed.).

Bukofzer, Manfred. 'Allegory in Baroque Music', *Journal of the Warburg Institute* III (1939).

Bulatkin, Eleanor W. 'The Arithmetical Structure of the O.F. *Vie de Saint Alexis*', *PMLA* LXXIV (1959).

—— *Structural Arithmetic. Metaphor in the Oxford 'Roland'* (Columbus, Ohio, 1972).

Butler, C. *Number Symbolism* (London, 1970).

—— See also under Fowler, Alastair (ed.).

Caird, J, B. *The Revelation of St John the Divine* (London, 1966).

Caldwell, John. See under Gibson, Margaret (ed.).

Candler, Howard. 'On the Symbolic Use of Numbers in the *Divina Commedia* and Elsewhere', *Transactions of the Royal Society of Literature,* Second Series XXX (1910).

Chadwick, Henry, *Boethius. The Consolations of Music, Logic, Theology and Philosophy* (Oxford, 1981).

Chapman, Coolidge Otis. 'Numerical Symbolism in Dante and *The Pearl*', *MLN* LIV (1939).

Craig, Hardin. *The Enchanted Glass: The Elizabethan Mind in Literature* (Stanford, 1935: Oxford, 1950).

Curtius, E. R. *Europäische Literatur und lateinisches Mittelalter* (Bern, 1948); trs. Willard R. Trask, *European Literature and the Latin Middle Ages* (London, 1953).

Davies, H. Neville. See under Fowler, Alastair (ed.) and Røstvig, Maren-Sofie (ed.).

Delany, Paul. See under Fowler, Alastair (ed.).

Duckworth, G. *Structural Patterns and Proportions in Vergil's Aeneid* (Ann Arbor, 1962).

Dunlop, Alexander. See under Fowler, Alastair (ed.).

Eaton, J. H. *Psalms. Introduction and Commentary* (London, 1967).

Eckhardt, Caroline D. (ed.). *Essays in the Numerical Criticism of Medieval Literature* (Lewisburg and London, 1980). Contents: Russell A. Peck, 'Number as Cosmic Language'; A. Kent Hieatt, 'Numerical Structures in Verse: Second-Generation Studies Needed (Exemplified in *Sir Gawain* and the *Chanson de Roland*)'; Charles S. Singleton, 'The Poet's Number at the Centre'; Elaine Scarry, 'The Well-Rounded Sphere: The Metaphysical Structure of *The Consolation of Philosophy*'; Allan Metcalf, 'Gawain's Number'; Caroline D. Eckhardt, 'The Number of Chaucer's Pilgrims: A Review and Reappraisal'; Thomas Elwood Hart, 'Tectonic Methodology and an Application to *Beowulf*'; Edward G. Fichtner, 'Patterns of Arithmetical Proportion in the *Nibelungenlied*'.

Festugière, A.-J. *La Révélation d'Hermès Trismégiste* (4 vols., Paris, 1950-1954).

Fichtner, Edward G. See under Eckhardt, Caroline D. (ed.).

Findlay, J. N. *Plato: The Written and Unwritten Doctrines* (London and New York, 1974).

Flegg, Graham. *Numbers: Their History and Meaning* (London, 1983).

Fowler, Alastair. *Spenser and the Numbers of Time* (London, 1964).

—— *Triumphal Forms: Structural Patterns in Elizabethan Poetry* (Cambridge, 1970).

—— *Conceitful Thought: The Interpretation of English Renaissance Poems* (Edinburgh, 1975).

—— (ed.), *Silent Poetry* (London, 1970). Contents: Christopher Butler, 'Numerological thought'; Maren-Sofie Røstvig, 'Structure as prophecy: the influence of Biblical exegesis upon theories of literary structure'; Russell A. Peck, 'Theme and number in Chaucer's *Book of the Duchess*'; A. Kent Hieatt, '*Sir Gawain:* pentangle, *luf-lace,* numerical structure'; Michael Baybak, 'Placement "in the middest" in *The Faerie Queene*'; Alexander Dunlop, 'The unity of Spenser's *Amoretti*'; Alastair Fowler, '"To Shepherd's ear": the form of Milton's *Lycidas*'; Alastair Fowler and Douglas Brooks, 'The structure of Dryden's *A Song for St Cecilia's Day, 1687*'; H. Neville Davies, 'The structure of Shadwell's *A Song for St Cecilia's Day, 1690*'; Douglas Brooks, 'Symbolic numbers in Fielding's *Joseph Andrews*'.

Gibson, Margaret (ed.). *Boethius: His Life, Thought and Influence* (Oxford, 1981). Contents include, John Caldwell, 'The De Institutione Arithmetica and the De Institutione Musica'; David Pingree, 'Boethius' Geometry and Astronomy'; Alison White, 'Boethius in the Medieval Quadrivium'.

Glasson, T. F. *The Revelation of John* (Cambridge, 1965).

Gombrich, E. II. *Symbolic Images: Studies in the Art of the Renaissance* (London and New York, 1972).

Guthrie, W. K. C. *The earlier Presocratics and the Pythagoreans (A History of Greek Philosophy I)* (Cambridge, 1962: paperback, 1978).

Hart, Thomas Elwood. See under Eckhardt, Caroline D. (ed.).

Hatcher, A. Granville. 'The Old French Poem *St Alexis:* A Mathematical Demonstration', *Traditio* 8 (1952).

Hatto, A. T. 'On Beauty of Numbers in Wolfram's Dawn Songs', *MLR* XLV (1950).

Haubrichs, Wolfgang. *Ordo als Form: Strukturstudien zur Zahlen-komposition bei Otfrid Weissenburg und in karolingische Literatur* (Tubingen, 1969).

Hellgardt, Ernst. *Zum Problem symbolbestimmter und formalästhetischer Zahlenkomposition in mittelaltericher Literatur* (Munich, 1973).

Hicatt, A. Kent. *Short Time's Endless Monument: The Symbolism of the Numbers in Edmund Spenser's 'Epithalamion* (New York, 1960).

—— 'The Daughters of Horus: Order in the stanzas of *Epithalamion*', in William Nelson (ed.), *Form and Convention in the Poetry of Edmund Spenser* (New York and London, 1961).

—— 'Arithmetic Metaphor in the *Roland*', *Medium Aevum* 43 (1974).

—— 'Symbolic and Narrative Patterns in *Pearl, Cleanness, Patience* and *Gawain*', *English Studiea in Canada* 2 (1976).

—— See also under Eckhardt, Caroline D. (ed.) and Fowler, Alastair (ed.).

—— and Constance Hieatt, '"The Bird with Four Feathers": Numerical Analysis of a Fourteenth-Century Poem', *Papers on Language and Literature* 6 (1970).

Hopper, Vincent. *Medieval Number Symbolism* (New York, 1938: reprinted Norwood, Pa., 1977).

Huisman, Johannes Alphonsus. *Neue Wege zur dichterischen und musikalischen Technik Walthers von der Vogelweide, mit einem Exkurs über die symmetrische Zahlenkomposition im Mittelalter* (Utrecht, 1950).

James, John. *The Ratio Hunter* (2nd ed., revised, Dooralong, 1978).

Kasmann, Hans. 'Numerical Structure in Fitt III of *Sir Gawain and the Green Knight*', in Beryl Rowland (ed.), *Chaucer and Middle English Studies in Honour of Rossell Hope Robbins* (London, 1974).

Klibansky, Raymond, Erwin Panofsky and Fritz Saxl. *Saturn and Melancholy: Studies in the History of Natural Philosophy, Religion and Art* (London, 1964).

Knowles, David. *The Evolution of Medieval Thought* (London, 1962).

Koenen, Ferdinand. 'Dantes Zahlensymbolik', *Deutsche Dante-Gesellschaft* VIII (1924).

Kristeller, Paul Oskar. *The Philosophy of Marsilio Ficino,* trs. Virginia Conant (New York, 1943: reprint, Gloucester, Mass., 1964).

Lausberg, H. 'Zum *Alexiuslied*', *Archiv für das Studium der neueren Sprachen* 191 (1955) and 195 (1958).

McKenzie, K. 'The Symmetrical Structure of Dante's *Vita Nuova*', *PMLA* XVIII (1903).

MacQueen, John. 'Saints' Legends and Celtic Life', *Folk Life* 5 (1967).

—— *Allegory* (London, 1970).

—— 'Neoplatonism and Orphism in Fifteenth-Century Scotland: the Evidence of Henryson's *New Orpheus*', *Scottish Studies* 20 (1976).

—— 'The literature of fifteenth-century Scotland', in Jennifer M. Brown (ed.), *Scottish Society in the Fifteenth Century* (London, 1977).

—— *Progress and Poetry* (Edinburgh, 1982).

Mâle, Émile. *L'Art religieux du XIIIe siècle en France: Étude sur l'iconographie du Moyen Age et sur ses source d'inspiration* (Paris, 1910); trs. Dora Nussey, *Religious Art in France, XIII Century: A Study in Medieval Iconography and its Sources of Inspiration* (London, 1913); reprint, *The Gothic Image: Religious Art in France of the Thirteenth Century* (paperback, London and Glasgow, 1961).

Masai, F. *Pléthon et le Platonisme de Mistra* (Paris, 1956).

Metcalf, Allan. See under Eckhardt, Caroline D. (ed.).

Meyer, Heinz. *Die Zahlenallegorese im Mittelalter: Methode und Gebrauch* (Munich, 1975).

Miskimin, Alice. 'Patterns in the *Kingis Quair* and Lydgate's *Temple of Glas*', *Papers on Language and Literature* 13 (1977).
—— 'The Design of Douglas's *Palice of Honour*', in J.-J. Blanchot and C. Graf (eds.), *Actes du 2 colloque de langue et de littérature écossaises* (*Moyen Age et Renaissance*) (Strasbourg, 1979).

Murray, Gilbert. *Five Stages of Greek Religion* (Oxford, 1925: Thinker's Library, 1935).

Norton, C. E. *The 'New Life' of Dante Alighieri* (Boston, Mass., 1859).

Patrides, C. A. (ed.). *The Cambridge Platonists* (London, 1969: paperback, Cambridge, 1980).

Panofsky, Erwin. See under Klibansky, Raymond.

Peck, Russell A. See under Eckhardt, Caroline D. (ed.) and Fowler, Alastair (ed.).

Peterson, R. G. 'Critical Calculations: Measure and Symmetry in Literature', *PMLA* 91 (1976).

Petrocchi, P. 'Del numero nel poema dantesco', *Rivista d'Italia* 111 (1901).

Pike, Lionel. *Beethoven, Sibelius and the Profound Logic* (London, 1978).

Pingree, David. See under Gibson, Margaret (ed.).

Qvarnström, Gunnar. *Dikten och den nya Vetenskapen. Det astronautiska motivet* (Lund, 1961).

Rabuse, Georg. *Der kosmische Aufbau der Jenseitsreiche Dantes* (Graz-Köln, 1958).

Reiss, Edmund. 'Number Symbolism and Medieval Literature', *Medievalia et Humanistica*, new series 1 (1970).

Robson, C. A. 'The Technique of Symmetrical Composition in Medieval Narrative Poetry', in E. A. Francis (ed.), *Studies in Medieval French Presented to Alfred Ewert* (Oxford, 1961).

Røstvig, Maren-Sofie. 'The Hidden Sense: Milton and the Neo-platonic Method of Numerical Composition', in *The Hidden Sense and Other Essays* (Oslo, 1963).
—— (ed.), *Fair Forms: Essays in English Literature from Spenser to Jane Austen* (Cambridge, 1975). Contents include, Einar Bjorvand, 'Spenser's defence of poetry: some structural aspects of the *Fowre Hymnes*'; Maren-Sofie Røstvig, 'Elaborate song: conceptual structure in Milton's "On the Morning of Christ's Nativity"', '*Tom Jones* and the Choice of Hercules'; H. Neville Davies, 'Laid artfully together: stanzaic design in Milton's "On the Morning of Christ's Nativity"', 'Dryden's Rahmenerzalung: the form of *An Essay of Dramatick Poesie*'.
—— See also under Fowler, Alastair (ed.).

Runciman, Sir Steven. *The Last Byzantine Renaissance* (Cambridge, 1970).

Saxl, Fritz. See under Klibansky, Raymond.

Scarry, Elaine. See under Eckhardt, Caroline D. (ed.).

Seznec, Jean. *La survivance des dieux antiques* (London, 1940); trs. Barbara F. Sessions, *The Survival of the Pagan Gods: The Mythological Tradition and its Place in Renaissance Humanism and Art* (New York, 1953; paperback, 1961).

Singleton, Charles S. *An Essay on the Vita Nuova* (Cambridge, Mass., 1949).

—— See also under Eckhardt, Caroline D. (ed.).

Smend, Friedrich. *Johann Sebastian Bach bei seinem Namen gerufen* (Kassel, 1950).

Stahl, William Harris. *Macrobius: Commentary on the Dream of Scipio* (New York and London, 1952).

Stevens, Denis and Alec Robertson. *Ancient Forms to Polyphony* (*Pelican History of Music I*) (Harmondsworth, 1960).

Taylor, A. E. *Plato: The Man and his Work* (London, 1926: paperback, 1960).

Welsford, Enid. *Spenser: Fowre Hymnes, Epithalamion* (Oxford, 1967).

White, Alison. See under Gibson, Margaret (ed.).

Whittaker, T. *The Neoplatonists* (2nd ed., Cambridge, 1918).

Wickert, Max A. 'Structure and Ceremony in Spenser's *Epithalamion*', *ELH* 35 (1968).

Wind, Edgar. *Pagan Mysteries in the Renaissance* (London, 1958: paperback, 1967).

Yates, Dame Frances A. *Giordano Bruno and the Hermetic Tradition* (London, 1964: paperback, 1978).

—— *The Art of Memory* (London, 1966: paperback, 1969).

Index

Abraham (Abram), 6, 7, 17, 51

Academy, Florentine, 101

Acrostics (alphabetical compositions), 1, 12-13, 49, 51-54
(compositions in which letters in initial and/or other regular positions make up words), 65-66

Acts of the Apostles, 114

Acts of John, 139

Adam, 51, 52, 79

Adam, J., 37, 38

Aeons, 138-139

Agar, 17

Agido, 131

Agrippa, Cornelius, 101, 102
De occulta philosophia, 102

Ailbe, Saint, 19, 20, 21, 23, 24

Alcman, 131
Partheneion, 131

Alexandria, 14

Alexis, Saint, 69, 71, 72

alpha (letter of Greek alphabet), 6, 13, 49, 51, 52, 53, 56, 66, 77

Alphabet, 5-13

Ambrosian Library (Milan), 55

Andrew, Saint, 65, 66

Angelic orders (hierarchy), 49, 52-53, 81, 88, 91, 93, 114, 511

Angels, angelic intelligences, 83, 88, 89-94, 102
Gabriel, 88, 89

Anima Mundi (Soul of the World), 31-36, 43-44, 48, 53, 103-105, 106, 108, 116

Antiphonary of Bangor, 55-57

Apollonius of Tyre, 128

Apparebit repentina (acrostic hymn), 49

Aquinas, Thomas, Saint, 90

Arabia, 17, 82

Arator, 17

Arcadius, emperor, 72

Aristotle, 94
Metaphysics, 94

arithmetic means, 34

Ark of the Covenant, 56

Ars Nova, 67

Artaxerxes, 9

Arthur, king, 72

Arts of Memory, 132, 134

Astrology, 28, 82

Athena (Pallas), 39, 62

Athenian Stranger (in Plato's *Laws* and *Epinomis*), 41

Atropos, 28

Augustine, Saint, of Hippo, 4, 10, 47, 48, 100, 102
City of God, 47, 48, 49

Aurora, 124

Bacchylides, 131

Bacon, Francis, 117

Badger in the Bag, 128

Baker, Herschel, 101

Bangor, 55, 56

Barinthus, Saint, 22

Barlaam of Calabria, 144

Barnabas, Saint, 109, 110

Melancholy, 120, 122, 123
Melias, Sir, 79
Memnon, 124
Mernoc, Saint, 22
Mesopotamia, 6, 69
Metres
  hexameter, 58, 65, 108, 110
  pentameter, 108, 110
  penthemimer, 58
  trimeter, 108
  tetrameter, 108
Milky Way (Watling Street),
  28, 30, 105
Milo of St Amand, 65, 69
  Life of St Amand, 65
Milton, John, 26, 100, 103,
  116, 117, 118, 121
  Comus, 124
  Il Penseroso, 103, 118–125
  L'Allegro, 103, 118–125
  Lycidas, 118, 123
  *On the Morning of Christ's
    Nativity*, 118
  Paradise Lost, 117, 118
  Poems (1645), 117
  Sonnet VII, 123
Minerva, 99, 112
Minnelieder, 66–67
Monad, 59, 112
Moses, 9, 10, 17, 19, 52, 56, 121
Murray, Gilbert, 5, 138
music, 27–28, 30–35, 42–43,
  45–46, 52, 55, 66–68, 80,
  103–104, 105, 106, 108, 116,
  120, 124
  cosmic, human and universal,
    46, 66

Nahor, 6
Nature (goddess), 95, 111, 114,
  116
*Navigatio Sancti Brendani
  Abbatis*, 18–25, 26, 55, 57, 69,
  72

Neale, J. M., 55
Necessity, Spindle of, 26–28
Nero, emperor, 8
New English Bible, 14
Newton, Isaac, 117
  *Principia mathematica philosophiae
    naturalis*, 117
Nicomachus of Gerasa, 45
  Introduction to arithmetic, 45
  Theological arithmetic, 45
Noah, 51, 57
Norton, C. E., 133
numbers, individual
  1   5, 21, 23, 29, 32, 33, 54, 55,
      59, 63, 73, 74, 76, 82, 86, 88,
      95, 96, 105, 115, 129, 144
  2   13, 15, 16, 17, 21, 23, 29, 30,
      32, 33, 34, 43, 44, 54, 55, 56,
      59, 61, 63, 73, 76, 78, 79, 80,
      84, 87, 88, 96, 105, 108, 115,
      125
  3   11, 13, 15, 16, 17, 20, 21, 22,
      23, 24, 28, 29, 30, 32, 33, 34,
      36, 37, 43, 50, 59, 60, 61, 63,
      64, 65, 73, 76, 78, 79, 81, 82,
      84, 87, 95, 96, 103, 104, 105,
      108, 109, 113, 115, 129, 130,
      144
  3½ 16
  4   11, 15, 16, 22, 23, 24, 29, 32,
      33, 34, 36, 36, 44, 50, 54, 55,
      56, 61, 63, 73, 76, 79, 80, 84,
      86, 88, 105, 115
  5   5, 7, 8, 17, 29, 37, 53, 63, 65,
      69, 70, 71, 72, 73, 74, 76, 78,
      79, 84, 96, 97, 103, 104, 105,
      131
  6   1, 11, 16, 17, 21, 22, 24, 29,
      32, 34, 51, 52, 55, 58, 59, 61,
      63, 79, 84, 85, 93, 96, 97,
      108, 110, 116, 133
  7   5, 11, 15, 16, 17, 22, 23, 24,
      29, 32, 38, 42, 43, 44, 55, 62,
      63, 64, 79, 80, 85, 87, 88, 95,